CW00969142

# The Politics of Profe

## Teachers and the Curriculum

*Gary McCulloch, Gill Helsby and Peter Knight*

CONTINUUM

London & New York

**Continuum**

Wellington House
125 Strand
London WC2R 0BB

370 Lexington Avenue
New York
NY 10017–6550

First published 2000

**British Library Cataloguing-in-Publication Data**
A catalogue record for this book is available from the British Library.

ISBN 0 8264 4814 3 (hardback)
    0 8264 4798 8 (paperback)

Typeset by York House Typographic Ltd, London
Printed and bound by Biddles Ltd, Guildford and King's Lynn

# Contents

# Preface and Acknowledgements

Professionalism is a crucial aspect of the work of teachers worldwide, and is much invoked but remains little understood. This book is an attempt to try to penetrate the myths that surround teacher professionalism and to understand both its limits and its possibilities, in the light of our engagement in international research and debate on the experience of teachers and schooling. It brings to a conclusion a research project that began in 1992, around the time of the British Conservative government's major report entitled *Choice and Diversity*, and ends in 1999, in the aftermath of the Labour government's report *Teachers: Meeting the Challenge of Change*. This has been a tumultuous period in schooling and in policy change, and we hope that the book reflects something of this extraordinary broader context.

This work is based principally on a research study funded by the Economic and Social Research Council entitled 'The Professional Culture of Teachers and the Secondary School Curriculum' (no. R000234738), which we refer to as the PCT study, based at Lancaster University (1994–6). We should like to thank the ESRC for its support for this project.

Gill Helsby, Peter Knight, Gary McCulloch and Murray Saunders were joint directors of the research project, and Terry Warburton was research associate. Murray Saunders and Terry Warburton were centrally involved in planning and conducting the research, but were not able to take part in preparing this book because of other commitments. We should like to take this opportunity to acknowledge our debt to their important contribution to the success of the project.

In preparing the present book, Gary McCulloch took the lead in drafting Chapter 1 and the chapters in Part 1. Gill Helsby and Peter Knight took the lead in drafting the chapters that make up Part 2. As joint authors we share responsibility for the work as a whole.

We should like to thank most sincerely the many teachers who gave so freely of their time to talk to us about their teaching, and also the key informants who took part in the study. The archives, professional associations and libraries that supported our study were also invariably helpful. Thanks should also go to the members of the many conferences and seminars where aspects of the current work were rehearsed and discussed, especially at the British Educational Research Association (1994 and 1996) and the American Educational Research Association (1993, 1995 and 1998), and for the international collaboration involved in the research network seminars of Professional Actions and Cultures of Teachers (PACT) (1993, 1995, 1997 and 1999). These have helped greatly to inform our understanding of teacher professionalism and of many other educational issues. We owe a special debt of gratitude to our colleagues in PACT, especially Ivor Goodson and Andy Hargreaves as the coordinators, and the organizer, Alicia Fernandez.

May we also thank the publishers for their commitment to this project, and especially Anthony Haynes for his enthusiasm and support.

Gary McCulloch
Gill Helsby
Peter Knight

# *Abbreviations*

| | |
|---|---|
| CACE | Central Advisory Council for Education |
| CSE | Certificate of Secondary Education |
| CSG | Curriculum Study Group |
| DES | Department of Education and Science |
| DFE | Department for Education |
| DfEE | Department for Education and Employment |
| ERA | Education Reform Act |
| ESRC | Economic and Social Research Council |
| GCE | General Certificate of Education |
| GCSE | General Certificate of Secondary Education |
| GMS | grant-maintained schools |
| HMI | Her Majesty's Inspector[ate] |
| INSET | in-service training |
| ITE | initial teacher education |
| LEAs | local education authorities |
| LMS | local management of schools |
| NAHT | National Association of Head Teachers |
| NCC | National Curriculum Council |
| NFER | National Foundation for Educational Research |
| NUT | National Union of Teachers |
| Ofsted | Office for Standards in Education |
| PACT | Professional Actions and Cultures of Teachers |
| PCT | Professional cultures of teachers research project |
| PRP | performance-related pay |
| QCA | Qualifications and Curriculum Authority |
| SATs | Standard Assessment Tasks |
| SCAA | School Curriculum and Assessment Authority |
| SSEC | Secondary Schools Examinations Council |
| *TES* | *The Times Educational Supplement* |
| TGAT | Task Group on Assessment and Testing |
| TTA | Teacher Training Agency |
| TVEI | Technical and Vocational Education Initiative |
| WO | Welsh Office |

# Chronology

| | |
|---|---|
| 1944 | Education Act |
| 1960 | Sir David Eccles (Minister of Education) 'Secret garden of the curriculum' speech |
| 1962 | Curriculum Study Group |
| 1964 | Schools Council established |
| 1976 | James Callaghan's Ruskin College speech – 'Great debate' |
| 1979 | Margaret Thatcher's Conservative government elected |
| 1982 | Schools Council abolished |
| 1983 | Launch of Technical and Vocational Education Initiative |
| 1985 | Government policy document *Better Schools* published. Teachers' Industrial action. |
| 1987 | Government consultation document on National Curriculum |
| 1988 | Education Reform Act; National Curriculum introduced. First orders for National Curriculum subjects appear and orders for all subjects are in place by 1991. Maths and technology curriculum requirements revised within two years of their introduction. |
| 1992 | Government policy document *Choice and Diversity* |
| 1993 | Teachers' action against testing for 7- and 14-year-olds |
| 1993–4 | Dearing Review of the National Curriculum and its assessment |
| 1995 | Introduction of new curriculum orders |
| 1997 | Tony Blair's Labour government elected |
| 1998 | Government consultation document *Teachers: Meeting the Challenge of Change* published. Proposals for introduction of 'literacy hour' and then 'numeracy hour' in primary schools. |
| 1999–2000 | Review of National Curriculum, leading to requirements for modest changes from September 2000. |

# Chapter 1

# Introduction

The Education Reform Act (ERA) of 1988, introduced by the British Conservative government of Margaret Thatcher, set in place wide-ranging reforms of schooling that many feared would end the notion of teachers as 'professionals'. In its stead, it was widely predicted that teachers would become mere technicians or functionaries, implementing orders that had been decided elsewhere. As recalled by *The Times Educational Supplement* (*TES*), the major British weekly newspaper for teachers, the ERA 'was loathed and resented by many, who saw it as a government attack on teachers' autonomy, integrity and professionalism' (*TES* 1998d). Among the measures introduced in the ERA was a highly prescriptive National Curriculum that laid down the content of the curriculum and standards of attainment for all pupils in state schools, from the start of their schooling at the age of five until the compulsory school leaving age of sixteen. It was this perhaps above all else that seemed to symbolize the death of teacher professionalism.

More than a decade after the ERA, the idea of teacher professionalism appears to have enjoyed a miraculous recovery in Britain, stimulated by the education policies of the new Labour government elected in 1997. The secretary of state for education and employment, David Blunkett, declared that 'professionalism is back at the very heart of teaching', as an integral part of the government's priority to raise standards and expectations for all pupils (Blunkett 1998). The prime minister, Tony Blair, made the first ever speech by a serving prime minister to a teacher union conference, delivered to the National Association of Head Teachers (NAHT) annual conference in Cardiff in June 1999, to underline his government's commitment to teachers' professionalism:

> The Government's objective is simple but highly ambitious. It is to restore teaching to its rightful place as one of Britain's foremost professions ... recognising the need for a step-change in the reputation, rewards and image of teaching, raising it to the status of other professions such as medicine and law, which are natural choices for our most able graduates.
> (Blair 1999)

But this would be a 'modernized' professionalism, very different from that of the past. It would make teachers responsible for improving standards for pupils, including those in socially disadvantaged areas. It would provide successful teachers with greater status and the most successful with higher salaries than they had received in the past. But it would bring penalties for those teachers and school principals who were unable or unwilling to rise to the challenge of raising standards as judged on the narrow definition of examination results. According to Blair, in his keynote speech to the Labour Party annual conference in 1998, 'If a headteacher rises to the challenge of turning round a failing school, why shouldn't they earn £60,000 to £70,000 a year? But equally if they cannot run the school properly, they shouldn't be running the school at all' (*TES* 1998b).

A consultative Green Paper was published in December 1998 to support these developments, advertised in advance by the prime minister as proposing 'the most fundamental reform of the teaching profession since state education began' (*TES* 1998b). This major policy document, entitled *Teachers: Meeting the Challenge of Change*, set out a case for 'modernising the teaching profession', and related this to an agenda of specific reforms. Chapter 1, 'The imperative of modernisation', underlined the need for schools to respond to major social and technological changes. This would entail in part the provision of new resources in the form of modern facilities for pupils and improved working conditions for teachers: 'The shabby staffroom and the battered electric kettle – which endured for so long because teachers always choose to put their pupils first – can become things of the past' (DfEE 1998, para. 9). At the same time, it would demand 'changes in the classroom', which would have 'profound implications' for teachers as individuals and for the profession as a whole: 'At the heart of what teachers do will remain the good, well-taught lesson – which has proved its effectiveness. But many new possibilities are emerging. Throughout this century teachers have had to choose between prioritising the needs of large groups or following up the diverse needs of individuals. Now for the first time they can realistically do both' (DfEE 1998, para. 5).

This in turn, according to the Green Paper, would mean teachers embracing a 'new professionalism'. It emphasized that this would not be a return to older notions of professionalism: 'The time has long gone when isolated, unaccountable professionals made curriculum and pedagogical decisions alone, without reference to the outside world' (DfEE 1998, para. 13). Instead, teachers would need to promote high expectations, to expect accountability, to take responsibility for improving their skills and subject knowledge, to seek to base decisions on evidence of what works in schools, to work in partnership with other staff in schools, to welcome the contribution of parents, business and others outside a school, to anticipate change, and to promote innovation (DfEE 1998, para. 13). They would require greater incentives for excellent performance, which again would challenge inherited ideals: 'The tradition in teaching is to treat all teachers as if their performance was similar, even though in every staffroom teachers themselves know this is not true' (DfEE 1998, para. 20). They would also need more systematic opportunities for their professional development. Most fundamentally of all, these aspirations would involve introducing a new staffing framework for schools that the Green Paper insisted would reward teachers for high performance and offer incentives for success.

The new government's ideas about a 'new professionalism' were echoed by senior executives responsible for managing and inspecting the education system. Chris Woodhead, the chief inspector of schools, argued that teachers should not be seen as 'mere technicians', and that teaching was not 'some kind of painting-by-numbers activity'

(*TES* 1998a). He emphasized what he saw as a new approach to teachers' profession-alism, moving away from a traditional concern with controlling the school curriculum, and towards issues relating to classroom practice, or pedagogy. This would not mean 'trying to define the way teachers should teach; it is not a toolkit approach'. He sought rather, through inspection reports for the Office for Standards in Education (Ofsted), to arm teachers with the knowledge that would allow them to make 'practical judg-ments on how to teach'. Ultimately, according to Woodhead, 'We need to move to a more outcome-based model of professionalism – to devolve as much as possible, and then to hold people accountable' (*TES* 1998a).

At the same time, Nicholas Tate, chief executive of the Qualifications and Curricu-lum Authority (QCA) insisted that the National Curriculum did not undermine the professionalism of teachers, but instead gave them the opportunity to enhance it. Tate pointed out that in France the existence of a national curriculum was taken for granted, but that it also allowed for reform of the school curriculum based on cultural, social and political aims. The lesson of this for the English education system, he suggested, was that while schoolteachers in England should have some autonomy, this should go together with a 'more explicit vision' for the curriculum as a whole than had so far been attained (Tate 1998). These principles would underlie a wide-ranging review of the National Curriculum during 1999, for implementation in the year 2000.

The nurturing of a new professionalism for teachers even proved attractive for the Conservative party, now in opposition, which had been responsible for the introduction of the National Curriculum. According to its new education spokesperson, David Willetts, the educational reforms of the Labour government were interfering with the professionalism of teachers. At the annual conference of the Conservative party in 1998, he urged that 'teachers should be given back their professionalism rather than having every minute of their teaching life micro-managed'. If teachers wanted to, he continued, they should be able to vote to become self-governing and set up their school as a workers' co-operative (*TES* 1998c). The imposition of what he called a 'command and control model' in which 'instructions flow down from the Department of Education and Employment to local authorities and schools as if they were junior outposts of a colonial administration' was, Willetts insisted, 'no way to raise educational standards and enhance the professionalism of teachers' (Willetts 1998, p. 13). According to Willetts's argument, higher standards and enhanced professionalism would be more likely if schools and teachers had greater freedom and autonomy rather than less.

The debate over teacher professionalism suggested in this set of interventions does more than demonstrate the return to favour in Britain of a term that had not too long since appeared hopelessly discredited and outmoded. It also reflects fierce contestation over the meaning of teacher professionalism and the kinds of approach that are needed in order to enhance it. The idea of 'professionalism' is politicized in this debate through its use as an instrument on behalf of different political interests. In this process, one theme that emerges with particular force is that an older tradition of teacher pro-fessionalism has been challenged with new notions of professionalism that threatened to supersede it. The conflict involved has not always been based on differences between political parties, although party-political differences have often been evident over this just as over other aspects of education especially in the past thirty years. Also, it has not always reflected overt ideological conflict, although again such conflict has been apparent in particular in the late 1980s and 1990s. No less significant than these more obvious forms of contestation have been more subtle processes of negotiation and mediation as teachers, policy-makers and other vested interests have sought to make sense of teacher professionalism during a period of rapid educational, social and political change.

This book tries to work towards an understanding of this debate around teacher professionalism in a range of connected ways. It traces the development of what we call the 'politics of professionalism' over the past fifty years, with special reference to secondary school teachers in England. Within this general aim, it seeks first to assess the nature of the impact of the National Curriculum in relation to secondary school teachers. Change is the most obvious feature of this impact, but we will also seek continuities over time and the tensions between change and continuity that are so often integral to phases of reform (McCulloch 1994). We will also seek to highlight the political characteristics of teacher professionalism over this time, before the Education Reform Act no less than since its inception.

In developing the present study, we have drawn on a wide range of published research into the nature of teachers' professionalism, the National Curriculum, and the policy context of the 1990s, and have attempted to build on it. Some of this previous research has suggested a rupture with the past. Lawn (1996) in particular suggests that 'the period between the 1920s and the 1990s constitutes a distinct phase in state education which has come to an end' (p. 1). He points to a major growth in differentiation between teachers, and argues strongly that the 'stability of the whole professional discourse' has been replaced by 'the built in instability of the constant restructuring of the transparent elements of their work' (p. 152).

On the other hand, some other commentators have indicated important ways in which teachers have mediated and adapted to the changes in their environment while at the same time maintaining key features of their established practice. According to Ball and Bowe, for example, 'The learning and changing that teachers and departments do in relation to the National Curriculum, like the learning that pupils do, involves making sense of the new in terms of past experiences and understandings' (1992, p. 103). Moreover, research on the impact of the Education Reform Act at Key Stage 1 (for 5- to 7-year-olds in primary schools) has suggested that while many teachers have been obliged to adopt new practices, this in itself would not necessarily change their values, and 'the exercise of coercive power has challenged some teachers to explore their professional repertoire in order to find ways in which they can mediate the new requirements or incorporate them into their existing practices' (Pollard *et al.* 1994, pp. 237–8). This kind of accommodation, involving a critical interaction with the challenge of innovation, has again been noted in recent research on the impact of the National Curriculum on play in reception classes (Wood 1999).

The recent collection of research on the relationship between teachers and the National Curriculum edited by Helsby and McCulloch (1997) sets out many of the issues that are also of prime concern for the present volume. This edited collection, which encompassed primary and secondary schools and a range of different subjects in the secondary school curriculum, showed how the National Curriculum has influenced the role of teachers in many important ways, but also suggested that teachers could often constrain, interpret and mediate the National Curriculum. The present book develops these points further with particular reference to teachers in secondary schools, especially for pupils over eleven up to the statutory leaving age of sixteen (Key

Stages 3 and 4 of the National Curriculum), to assess the extent to which there has been a fundamental shift in principles and precepts in this sector of education.

In the current work we are also strongly conscious of issues about the character of 'professional knowledge' and how this impinges on the professionalism of teachers. The ideas of Donald Schön in particular, developing the notion of the 'reflective practitioner', have been a potent influence over the past decade, with a key argument being that 'technical rationality' is not sufficient as a basis for professional practice (Schön 1983). Useful critiques of Schön's arguments have also emerged during the 1990s (for example Eraut 1994), with the result that a debate over how to understand the nature of teachers' professional knowledge provides an important set of influences for our own research (see also Hoyle and John 1995).

The international and indeed global relationships involved in our work should also be noted at this stage. During the 1990s there has been some important research in different national and cultural contexts on the nature of teacher professionalism, notably under the auspices of the international research network Professional Actions and Cultures of Teachers (PACT), in which we have also been involved. Major collections of research that have resulted from this collaboration strongly indicate a general movement towards state control and greater teacher accountability, while at the same time reflecting a continuing discourse around teacher professionalism (see for example Goodson and Hargreaves 1996; Shimahara 1998; Day *et al.* 1999). In an important sense we would want to situate our work within this wider range of research, as an example of how teachers' professionalism has struggled to survive and has developed in new directions amid the conflicts of the 1990s.

The broader importance of teacher professionalism in sociological and socio-historical terms establishes a further set of frameworks for this present study. Exploring the nature of teachers' professionalism is not simply an exercise in labelling teaching as a profession, an art, a craft or a technology. Viewed as such, it might quickly become a recondite study of purely academic value. The professional standing of teachers and teaching has deeper implications than this would imply, for instance as a means of assessing the nature of socio-political change. Sociologists in general are interested in the distribution of wealth, power, authority and status within society, and in the ways in which these distributions are maintained, contested and changed. For them, the case of the status of teaching, the ways in which that status alters, and the ways in which different groups are affected by the struggles for status and control, are of considerable, wider interest. Moreover, teachers' representatives, such as teachers' unions, have a direct interest in understanding the range of realities and myths of teachers' work. Representing teachers well depends on knowing how they experience their work and how they feel about it. The same is true for those who wish to change teachers' work. Innovators who misunderstand that which they seek to change are vulnerable innovators. The education, treatment and rewards of teachers are all related to the ways in which the occupation is seen. In short, the view of teaching is central to the way that action is taken to maintain and enhance the quality of children's learning.

Teaching is clearly an occupation, but is it a profession? And if so, what makes it one? An approach to these questions would have been to survey the literature (which was done) and, through the application of critical thinking, to arrive at a set of characteristics or traits that characterize a profession. This kind of 'trait theory' has a long history, and is the default option in the study of professions. However, it is apparent that there is disagreement about which traits do define a profession as well as about their relative importance. These traits are often little more than descriptions of medicine and law, explicitly so in the case of Prime Minister Blair's speech to the NAHT that has already been quoted. However, on this basis many avowedly 'professional' occupations do not seem to have enough defining traits to be considered as professions. Indeed, there is little agreement on which traits are the most important and how many are needed before an occupation can be seen as a major profession, a minor profession, a semi-profession, or whatever.

In sum, this trait approach to identifying professional occupation is open to at least six objections. First, it is assumed that the occupations of medicine and law are homogenous, with the result that practitioners who work in large law firms or within hospitals and community health organizations are ignored, since their work is not marked by the same traits, to the same degree, as the work of independent practitioners. Second, it ignores the way that professionals in continental Europe frequently work in bureaucracies. Third, it is unclear whether all the defining traits need to be present for an occupation to be regarded as a profession, and whether some are necessary and others are simply supplementary evidence. Fourth, it is blind to common, everyday usage of the term 'profession'. Fifth, it is unhistorical, failing to recognize that what is recognized as a profession in one place and time is not accepted in another. And sixth, it makes it seem as though there is an uncontentious and value-free way of identifying professional occupations. There is no such way, nor can there be. 'Profession' is a socially constructed, dynamic and contested term.

An alternative approach derives from this last point and is tantamount to claiming that a profession is any occupation that is accepted as a profession. At first sight this approach has a certain elegance to it, for it allows 'professions' to be readily identified by simple empirical terms, such as surveys of public opinion. Yet the public does not speak with one voice. However professions are identified, it is clear that the term represents judgements that are specific to times and contexts, and that they are judgements that also reflect the different stances of different people and groups in society.

In documenting these issues, the book is divided into two general parts. The first is devoted to long-term frameworks, assessing changes and continuities over more than fifty years since the Second World War. We review the ways in which teacher professionalism has developed especially from public and official perspectives: the ideals involved, the myths and memories that it cultivated, and the political arguments and debates that revolved around it. These will be assessed mainly through recourse to documentary sources such as policy reports, the printed media and (for the period from the 1940s to the 1960s) primary sources held at the Public Record Office, although oral testimony provided by teachers and policy-makers in the 1990s also provides valuable evidence of change over this longer term. In the second main part of the book, we focus more on medium- and short-term frameworks over the past decade, enabling us to look more closely at the views of teachers and of key policy-makers and opinion-formers during this period, and also to relate these in more detail to the broader contexts of policy 'reform' (Helsby 1999) in the 1990s. This second section is based more fully on a range of oral evidence amassed during the past decade, especially from a major study funded by the Economic and Social Research Council (ESRC) on the professional cultures of teachers (PCT). Details of the samples of teachers and policy-makers involved in the PCT study are to be found in an Appendix.

Relating the primary documentary sources to the oral evidence has not been a straightforward exercise. The primary documentary sources, mainly held at the Public Record Office in Kew, provide important clues to the development of policy and interactions and tensions among interest groups. In most cases they are also subject to the 'Thirty Year Rule' that prevails in the United Kingdom in relation to official records, and so for the purposes of the current study they are most helpful for the 1950s and 1960s. The oral evidence, on the other hand, gives suggestive insights into the thinking of practising teachers and of a range of key policy-makers and opinion-formers in the 1990s. The combination of these two sets of evidence allows us to relate overarching policy trends in teacher professionalism over the past fifty years to a more detailed study of teachers' attitudes in the 1990s. They do not allow us very far into teachers' thinking in the 1950s and 1960s, or into policy debates behind the scenes since the 1970s. Each of these important issues should form the basis for continuing research in future years. The current work sets out a provisional framework and an agenda for such work as it investigates continuity, change and conflict in the politics of teacher professionalism in the past half-century. In doing so, it poses two central questions for discussion: what is the nature of teachers' professionalism, and how has it changed in the last decade?

*Part 1*

---

# The Secret Garden

# *Introduction*

In the House of Commons debate in March 1960 on the recently published Crowther Report, *15 to 18*, the then minister of education, Sir David Eccles, made a comment that at the time attracted relatively little comment, but which came in time to symbolize an entire era. Eccles remarked that the report's findings on sixth forms were 'an irresistible invitation for a sally into the secret garden of the curriculum' (*Hansard* 1960). He continued:

> I regret that so many of our education debates have had to be devoted almost entirely to bricks and mortar and to the organisation of the system. We hardly ever discuss what is taught to the 7 million boys and girls in the maintained schools. We treat the curriculum as though it were a subject, like the other place [i.e. the House of Lords], about which it is 'not done' for us to make remarks. I should like the House to say that this reticence has been overdone.

Of course, Eccles quickly added, 'Parliament would never attempt to dictate the curriculum'. Nevertheless, 'from time to time, we could with advantage express views on what is taught in schools and training colleges'. He concluded: 'I shall, therefore, try in the future to make the Ministry's own voice heard rather more often, more positively, and, no doubt, sometimes more controversially' (*Hansard* 1960).

Eccles's statement in the Commons has become emblematic for two basic reasons. First, it evoked the general orthodoxy of the period, roughly from the Second World War until the 1970s, that teachers should be virtually autonomous in the curriculum domain, and that the curriculum was therefore a matter neither for public debate nor for state involvement. Second, it contains a predictive message that this would not always be the case which anticipates the very different orthodoxy of the 1980s and 1990s. His comment that 'Parliament would never attempt to dictate the curriculum' adds an ironic twist that allows us, forty years later, to understand both the prevailing mentality of the 1960s and the profound changes that have taken place in the decades that followed.

The first part of this book tries to take us behind Eccles's familiar statement to the assumptions and relationships that developed in the 'secret garden'. It highlights the strength of a 'myth' or 'tradition' of teacher professionalism that was current especially in the 1950s and 1960s. It explores the differences between the ideal of teacher professionalism that developed in this period and the complex realities that underlay and often contradicted it. It also seeks to trace the legacy of these assumptions in the debates of the 1980s–90s and the extent of their enduring resonance. This first part, therefore, is an attempt to address key phenomena relating to teachers in a diachronic rather than a synchronic manner. That is, it charts their development over time, as opposed to examining them without taking into account their historical origins and precedents. However, the treatment is not strictly chronological, but consists of overlapping analyses of different features that each shed light on teachers and their professionalism.

Chapter 2 investigates the ideal of teacher professionalism that flourished in the 1950s and 1960s, and tries to understand the way in which a tradition or 'myth' was established in these years. It goes on to survey in general and introductory terms the defence of this ideal in changing circumstances in the 1980s and 1990s, and to suggest the significance of its legacy for an understanding of the debates of these years.

In Chapter 3 we return to the 1950s and 1960s to study in detail some of the ways in which often fierce disputes developed behind the façade of consensus. The public orthodoxy of teacher autonomy and control allowed scope for negotiation over what this should entail and how to promote it in the face of impending threats. Exploring these arenas of debate reminds us that the nature of teacher professionalism was always problematic and fragile even in this era when it seems outwardly to have been at its strongest, and that it was endangered by educational and social factors that were potent in this particular historical context.

Chapter 4 examines the assumptions of the 'secret garden' from another perspective, that provided by the memories of teachers and policy-makers in the 1990s. Confronted by a new and changing environment, these teachers and policy-makers drew on their memories and experiences of the past to help provide their bearings for the future. Hansot and Tyack, in the United States, have argued that 'Present actions and plans for the future flow ineluctably from beliefs about what went before' (1982, p. 21). This chapter attempts to reconstruct these beliefs about the nature of the 'secret garden', and how they helped to influence attitudes to the changes that were going on around them.

Taken as a whole, Part 1 is a portrait of the 'secret garden' that tries to visualize both its general landscape and its hidden undergrowth. In so doing, it reconstructs a set of values and assumptions about teacher professionalism that were specifically associated with a particular social and educational context. It is these that form our key point of reference before we proceed in Part 2 of our study to investigate in more detail the challenges and changes that arose in the final decade of the twentieth century.

# Chapter 2

# An 'English Tradition' of Teacher Professionalism

Ideals of teacher professionalism in the English context have been closely associated with the assumption that teachers should control the curriculum, that is, what they teach and how they teach it. This reflects a potent historical tradition of teacher autonomy in the curriculum domain. In this chapter, we will investigate the character of this distinctive historical tradition, and then assess its continuing relevance in the rapidly changing educational and political circumstances of the 1990s.

At first sight, it may seem unlikely that a particularly strong tradition of this kind should have developed in this particular educational and social context. In the nineteenth century, after all, elementary school teachers in England and Wales were allowed very little freedom in the curriculum domain. The Revised Code of 1862 was notorious for the restrictions that it set upon the effective role of teachers (Sylvester 1969). The comments of Robert Lowe, a leading educational administrator of the 1860s, reflected a deeply ingrained assumption: 'Teachers desiring to criticise the Code were as impertinent as chickens wishing to decide the sauce in which they would be served' (Lawton 1980, p. 16). There have been echoes of this general attitude during the twentieth century also, especially since the introduction of a National Curriculum under the Education Reform Act of 1988.

On the other hand, it has often been noted that in the 1940s and 1950s teachers enjoyed an unusual degree of latitude in curriculum matters. For example, Denis Lawton has argued that the period from the Education Act of 1944 until the beginning of the 1960s marked 'the Golden Age of teacher control (or non-control) of the curriculum' (Lawton 1980, p. 22). Lawton's view is that during this period, 'teachers had their chance to take control of the curriculum, but failed to take it' (*ibid.*). It is important to establish how far the expectations raised at that time have asserted a continuing force and relevance since the 1960s. The series of major incursions into the curriculum field on the part of the state that has developed over that time, together with the systematic undermining of teachers' independence in the name of 'accountability', might be judged to have created wholly new circumstances in which earlier assumptions are rendered irrelevant and out of date. Thus, according to Martin Lawn,

> In retrospect, teacher autonomy as an exploratory idea in curriculum control in England and Wales may now be seen as historically specific to the period 1925–80 . . . In recent years a shift in educational policy and a return to overt, centralised administrative controls in education have muted or replaced this once common explanation in the curriculum field of autonomy, professionalism and partnership.                    (Lawn 1987a, p. 227)

A third issue that needs to be borne in mind in such a discussion is the problematic nature of the idea of 'professionalism' in relation to teachers. The notion of professionalism is beset with conceptual difficulties and ambiguities, to such an extent as even to raise questions over its value as a tool of analysis. Freidson, a leading sociological commentator on the professions, suggests that 'The concrete, historical character of the concept and the many perspectives from which it can legitimately be viewed, and from which sense can be made of it, preclude the hope of any widely accepted definition of general analytical value' (1994, p. 27). So far as teachers are concerned, it is further undermined by official discourses of teacher professionalism that often lack any clear meaning or else may be read in several different ways at the same time, for example in the multiple simultaneous readings propounded in the White Paper *Better Schools* in 1985:

> Like other professionals, teachers are expected to carry out their professional tasks in accordance with their judgment, without bias, precisely because they are professionals. This professionalism requires not only appropriate training and experience but also the professional attitude which gives priority to the interests of those served and is constantly concerned to increase effectiveness through professional development.(DES 1985, p. 44)

In order to begin to decode such usages, it is important to attempt to locate the idea of teacher professionalism in relation to changing historical, political and social contexts. Its meanings have adapted and developed over time and in contestation between rival groups and interests. It needs also to be understood as a form of ideology, one that has helped to legitimize controls over teachers but has also provided them with some autonomy of their own. As Ozga has observed, teacher professionalism constitutes 'a concept of considerable resonance for teachers, one which both incorporates them into state service, and yet gives them the strength to resist external controls' (Ozga 1992, p. 7).

It is useful also to make a basic distinction between the ideas of 'professionalism' and 'professionalization' in relation to teachers. In the United States, Linda Eisenmann has suggested that whereas professionalization denotes issues of status, professionalism concerns the rights and obligations of teachers to determine their own tasks in the classroom, that is, how teachers use their own knowledge (Eisenmann 1991). This distinction seems particularly apt in the English context. The idea of professionalization is highly familiar in the historical literature as a political project on the part of teachers to be publicly acknowledged as 'professionals', and of teachers' unions and associations to establish teaching as a recognized 'profession' on the same level as, for example, medicine or law.

The classic works on teachers' history emphasized what they perceived as the 'growth of a profession'. Asher Tropp (1957), for example, sought to document the 'growth of the teaching profession' by investigating the historical role of the National Union of Teachers in establishing a gradual rise in 'professional status'. The major achievements that are viewed as relevant to this process include the development of qualifications, the exclusion of uncertificated teachers, the improvement of conditions of work, the obtaining of security of tenure, clear provision for promotion to higher ranks, salary and pension schemes, increased influence and importance as a professional group, the growing trust of parents, increasing unity among teachers' groups, and the creation of a more favourable image for teachers and their unions. Tropp's work also reflects a liberal model of gradual progress and improvement in teachers' development towards public esteem in relation to other occupational groups, as it concludes: 'The position of the school teachers could well be regarded by other professions and would-be professions. Without any of the advantages of the older professions, they have fought successfully for the welfare of the schools and for an increase in their status' (Tropp 1957, p. 270). The role of teachers in the classroom, or of their relationship to the school curriculum, finds very little place in this discussion. Similarly, Peter Gosden's account of the 'contribution of teachers' associations to the development of school teaching as a professional occupation' stressed the importance of reaching 'a reasonable level of salaries, pensions, security of tenure, sound training and qualifications and some recognition by the community of the profession's right to influence the way in which the service it offers is administered' (Gosden 1972, Foreword).

More recent research has developed this general line of argument without necessarily sharing in the liberal assumptions about gradual progress that had been so strong. The struggle of women teachers and their associations for increased security and status has been well documented (e.g. Widdowson 1983). The means by which teachers' groups enhanced their public status through channels such as the media have also attracted greater attention (e.g. Cunningham 1992). There has also developed a powerful counter-argument that has contradicted the notion of professional aspirations and instead emphasized the idea of teachers as workers, highlighting the importance of class solidarity and industrial action in relation to teachers (e.g. Lawn 1987b). This kind of debate has reflected strong tensions between teachers' trade-unionism and their professional aspirations, often observed in the views of teachers themselves (e.g. Ginsburg *et al.* 1980; Pietrasik 1987) and exploited in negotiations by local and state authorities. Thus for example John Patten, when secretary of state for education in the 1990s, drew a clear distinction between 'teachers I meet in the classroom, or heads I meet for informal discussions', and the role of teacher trade unions that 'face in the direction of pay and conditions on the one hand – sometimes merging into militancy – and serious discussion of professional issues on the other'. According to Patten, 'It is perfectly proper for people to form themselves into associations to bargain over pay and conditions .... But I do not think that the professionalism of teachers is helped by them even being identified as "unions" ' (*The Independent* 1993a).

Patten's use of the term 'professionalism' here obscures the very different way in which an ideal of professionalism has tended to develop for teachers in England and Wales, relating in particular to a supposed position of control and autonomy in the curriculum domain. This ideal again has some basis in sociological literature on the professions. Freidson's research on the medical profession, for example, suggests that a profession is an occupation that gains control over the 'determination of the substance of its own work' (Freidson 1970, p. xvii) so that it becomes autonomous or self-directing. Whatever other kinds of control are exercised over a professional group by the state, Freidson contends, 'so long as a profession is free of the technical evaluation and control of other occupations in the division of labour, its lack of ultimate freedom from the state, and even its lack of control over the socio-economic terms of work do not significantly change its essential character as a profession' (1970, p. 25). Central to 'professional autonomy', on Freidson's definition, is 'sufficient authority over work to be free to take discretionary action as a matter of course' (Freidson 1994, p. 166). Torstendahl also emphasizes the importance to professional groups of exercising control over a knowledge base, and similarly warns that such control 'has never been characterised by a total autonomy' (Torstendahl 1990, p. 5). Rather, he argues, professional groups 'are granted "jurisdiction" of their problem area by their employers, collaborators, clients or indirect financers (the taxpayers in many cases) which can be withdrawn or changed in scope when the surroundings demand a change' (1990, p. 5). The ideal of teacher professionalism, especially for secondary school teachers, has drawn on this kind of concept of discretion and jurisdiction within a defined area of knowledge. A key area for debate has therefore been the school curriculum and the scope and limitations of teachers in defining their knowledge base, or what they can teach, and how to teach it.

## IDEALS OF TEACHER PROFESSIONALISM

In the context of England and Wales, the ideal of teacher professionalism as curriculum control was identified as a key defining feature especially from the 1940s onwards. It was developed for social and political reasons as a phenomenon that was integral to a 'national tradition', marking a decisive difference between state education in England and Wales and that in other nations and cultures. In a changing social and political context over the following half-century, this ideal came under increasing threat, and was vigorously contested especially over the implications of a National Curriculum imposed by the state.

Traditions, whether they are comparatively recent in origin or of long standing, are often invented for social and political purposes (Hobsbawm and Ranger 1983). They also tend to be based on 'myth', a notion that can be used in two basic and distinct senses. On the one hand, myth can underpin a Marxist notion of ideology by which ideas are considered as 'manifestations of certain group interests, practical instruments whereby social classes and other sections of the community uphold their own interests and values' (Kolakowski 1978, p. 155). It has often been employed in this sense by Marxist thinkers who have shown its importance as a device for maintaining power, authority and domination over groups that might otherwise be unwilling to accept their place in society. On the other, it can evoke an overarching purpose or aim that, irrespective of its relation to truth or reality, helps to sustain a mission, image or system. This latter approach has its roots in anthropology, for example in the work of Malinowski (Strenski 1992), which has documented the cultural importance of myth in establishing and maintaining group identity.

In relation to education, national traditions have exerted an important influence upon the character of educational change. In Scotland, for example, as R. D. Anderson has convincingly argued, an 'advanced and distinctive' educational tradition provided a tangible link with the past that gave in turn 'a point of superiority over England and a guarantee of Scotland's social and cultural autonomy within the Union' (Anderson 1983, p. 1). Indeed, according to Anderson,

> The belief that Scottish education was peculiarly 'democratic', and that it helped to sustain certain correspondingly democratic features of Scottish life, formed a powerful historical myth, using that word to indicate not something false, but an idealization and distillation of a complex reality, a belief which influences history by interacting with other forces and pressures, ruling out some developments as inconsistent with the national tradition, and shaping the form in which the institutions inherited from the past are allowed to change.
> (Anderson 1983, p. 1).

In many respects, as Anderson allows, there is a mismatch between the 'ideal' symbolized in the national tradition and the 'reality' as experienced by particular individuals and groups. In spite of this kind of tension, on the other hand, the 'democratic myth' could continue to maintain a 'shaping influence' on the character of change, even to the extent that it might become 'a substitute for hard thinking about contemporary problems'. For example, Anderson suggests, 'constant and complacent assertions that Scottish education was democratic might cover its actual evolution on class lines' (Anderson 1983, p. 26).

The notion of an 'educational myth' has also been emphasized by C. E. Beeby, director of education in New Zealand from 1940 until 1960. Beeby interprets this in terms of an overarching idea about the purposes of education, expressing a particular intention or orientation. He suggests several key characteristics to such myths. First, they should be in general accord with some strong, although not always clearly defined, public aspiration. Second, the language in which they are expressed must be 'flexible enough to permit a reasonably wide range of interpretations, and yet specific enough to provide practical guidance to administrators, planners and teachers'. They need also to be 'unattainable' at least in the immediate future, so as to provide an ideal of the future for a generation of educators. Beeby adds that by the time it is close enough to be seen clearly, the 'weaknesses' of a myth will also become apparent, and 'a rival myth will be edging its way into the centre of vision'. Moreover, he concludes, 'the key people working under the myth must believe in it so completely that they will fight for it in its youth (while perhaps in their youth); must hold on to it, though more critically, in its middle age, and yet eventually be willing to see another myth set up in its place when it has served its purpose' (Beeby 1989, pp. xv–xvi). It is noticeable that whereas the kind of national tradition that Anderson depicts has the historic past as its reference point, Beeby emphasizes aspirations for the future. Such traditions nevertheless imply both a belief in a 'golden past' and faith in an idealized future (see also McCulloch 1995b).

Notions of an 'English tradition' in education have been similarly employed to inform and justify specific forms of outlook, planning or policy. In the nineteenth century, public schools and universities confirmed their pre-eminence as 'defining institutions', and thus their public authority and status in relation to other types of educational institutions, partly through recourse to a socially and politically acceptable notion of their traditions (Steedman 1987; McCulloch 1988). In the 1920s, Cyril Norwood, Head of Harrow School, attempted to articulate and defend an 'English tradition of education' in terms of the espoused values and ethos of the independent 'public' schools (Norwood 1929; see also McCulloch 1991, esp. chs 3–4). Welsh traditions tended to be subsumed and incorporated within the English, although increasingly resistance and dissent manifested themselves in distinct notions of a Welsh culture and identity (e.g. Webster 1990). After the Second World War, the Education Act of 1944 became established as a characteristic symbol of an English tradition that was reconstructed for the purposes of the post-war 'Welfare State' (McCulloch 1994, ch. 4), while proposed innovations such as comprehensive schools for all abilities and aptitudes were often criticized for failing to accord with the established English 'social tradition' (Dent 1952, p. 11). Over the past fifty years, notions of a distinctive English tradition have often reasserted themselves in the face of challenges either internal or external. As Goodson argues, the National Curriculum itself may be read as a major initiative to rebuild the nation-state and to re-establish national identity and ideology, in response to fears of economic decline, cultural dissolution and a loss of national power (Goodson 1994, ch. 7). And yet in another way the significance of the National Curriculum lay in the series of challenges that it posed to another socially constructed national tradition, the idea of teacher professionalism defined in terms of autonomy and effective control in the curriculum domain, which had become established earlier in the century.

Gerald Grace's notion of 'legitimated professionalism' provides a socio-historical model that strongly evokes this earlier phase of relative curricular freedom. Grace suggests that in the 1950s and 1960s, an educational settlement between teachers and the state gave rise to considerable professional autonomy in relation to the curriculum despite setbacks in teachers' terms and conditions of service, to the extent that

> In contrast to highly centralised and controlled systems of state schooling in other socio-political contexts, the decentralised autonomy of British teachers with respect to curriculum selection and pedagogic methods was taken to be a distinctive feature of British democracy and schooling.                                   (Grace 1987, p. 212)

This ideal of autonomy was related to a notion of 'partnership' between teachers, local education authorities (LEAs), and the state in the development of the education service. It was also a key aspect of the ideal of education as a civic project that was cultivated at this time. In contrast and opposition to the trend of the fascist and authoritarian states, the independence of teachers was emphasized over and above aspirations to promote particular ideas such as 'education for citizenship' (see McCulloch 1994, ch. 6). Maurice Holmes, permanent secretary at the Ministry of Education, noted in 1945 that 'This Department is under constant pressure to secure that this or that subject is included in the curriculum of schools.' He preferred what he called the 'traditional and, I think, wholesome practice' in which 'We have always resisted such proposals on the ground that in this country the details of the curriculum are not controlled or directed by the Ministry but are left to the determination of the LEAs and the teachers' (Holmes 1945).

Whatever the variations between the 'ideal' and the 'reality' (and we will explore these in some detail in Chapter 3), the tradition of teacher professionalism in this particular sense became well established during this period. As J. F. Kerr, professor of education at the University of Leicester, insisted in the late 1960s, 'The teachers worked hard to achieve some degree of professional autonomy and by the 1950s it was generally accepted they were free to decide what and how they should teach' (Kerr 1968, p. 13). It also represented a distinctive feature of an English tradition as distinct from that of other cultures and nations. Stuart Maclure, editor of the *TES*, observed at an international conference on 'curriculum innovation in practice' held in 1967 that the English delegates reacted against the abstractions and theories developed elsewhere, especially in the United States, by turning 'with relief' to the 'nuts and bolts of curriculum reform and in particular to the English myth of the autonomy of the teacher as master of his fate and his pupils' curriculum' (Schools Council 1968, p. 10). According to Maclure, this was a myth 'in the sense that it expresses great truths in a form which corresponds more to an idea than to reality'. Thus, Maclure asserted,

> Throughout the conference this tended to be the characteristic English contribution – to concentrate attention on the teacher, his role as a professional who must be directly implicated in the business of curriculum renewal; not as a mere purveyor of other people's bright ideas, but as an innovator himself. To refer to this as a myth is not to denigrate it. It is a crucial element in the English educational idea. (Schools Council 1968, p. 10)

The chief education officer for the West Riding, Sir Alec Clegg, for example, described his ideal 'teacher of the future' as 'a professional making his own diagnoses and prescribing his own treatments', rather than 'a low-grade technician working under someone else's instructions' (Schools Council 1968, p. 25).

Similarly, it was widely assumed that teachers would be consulted on broad policy issues relating to education. During the reorganization of secondary education in the mid-1960s under the Labour government of Harold Wilson, teachers' groups and organizations were prominent in asserting their interests. The president of the National Union of Teachers, Miss Stewart, insisted in uncompromising terms in November 1964 that teachers 'had a right to be consulted on schemes affecting their professional status and livelihood' (DES 1964). Moreover, she added, 'They welcomed the increasing public interest in education, but it was not all well informed and they believed that their opinion should be a fundamental consideration in educational matters.' This, she insisted, was basic to their professionalism, which should be respected just as much as that of the recognized professions: 'It was difficult to imagine any other professional area in which so little attention would be paid to practitioners' views.' If her concern here was about teachers' public project of professionalization, however, it quickly reverted to the familiar focus of the curriculum domain, as she concluded: 'Teachers should retain their full right to determine the curriculum' (DES 1964).

In Anderson's terms, teacher professionalism can here be understood in terms of a powerful 'historical myth', not necessarily to imply something false but 'an idealization and distillation of a complex reality' (Anderson 1983, p. 1). Whatever the limits of teacher control over the curriculum may have been in reality, and these were in fact considerable, the myth presupposed the existence of what David Eccles described most succinctly as a 'secret garden' in which teachers went virtually unrestrained in the exercise of their autonomy. It also represented an ideal that its adherents fiercely defended when it was challenged, and especially in the face of increasingly explicit and powerful threats against its integrity from the 1970s onwards.

## CONTESTING TEACHER PROFESSIONALISM

By the mid-1980s a massive incursion on the part of the state into the curriculum domain appeared to many observers to have decisively undermined this ideal of teacher professionalism. This view can lead to a straightforward notion of the erosion and eventual collapse of teacher control and autonomy in the area of the curriculum in the face of state involvement, with the National Curriculum representing the logical final stage in this long-term process that fatally compromised teachers' claims to professional standing. It is possible, however, to interpret the developing relationship between teachers and the curriculum in more problematic terms, again in relation to its long-term historical context. An emphasis on the idea of contestation suggests not a simple model of the decline of teachers' influence, but a framework that involves continuing debate among teachers and other groups and interests, including the agencies of the state. In particular, the myth of teacher professionalism established earlier in the twentieth century has been challenged and defended over the past two decades during a major cycle of rapid educational policy change, and during this process continued to exercise an important influence over the nature of these developments.

In October 1976, the then prime minister James Callaghan launched what was described as a 'Great Debate' on education with a major speech delivered at Ruskin College, Oxford. This was greeted with alarm by many sympathizers of teachers and local education authorities (Chitty 1989). When the Conservative party was elected to office under Margaret Thatcher at the general election of 1979, consternation was quickly replaced by dismay. The NUT now took strong exception to any apparent shifts in education policy, and did so by drawing heavily on the established ideals with which teachers had been identified over the previous generation. For instance, it expressed strong dissent from the philosophy of the DES Circular 14/77, and the Welsh Office Circular 185/77, on curriculum content and the means of determining the curriculum. According to Dr Walter Roy, on behalf of the NUT,

> The central issue in curriculum determination was the availability of resources and ... his organisation took the view that the Government should stop publishing documents of a prescriptive nature, which were incompatible with a local service.          (DES 1979)

It was equally significant however that the DES did not at this stage accept that a basic shift in education policy was taking place. The 'English tradition' of teacher professionalism continued to be viewed as the starting point and key basis for discussion. Therefore a senior DES official responded to the NUT's criticisms by suggesting that government participation in curriculum matters did not represent a departure from this orthodoxy, since:

> Curricular decisions were required at both central and local government level as well as by the schools; central and local government could not carry out their work except on the basis of certain curricular assumptions and policies but this did not diminish – nor was it incompatible with – the role of teachers in schools.          (DES 1979)

Teachers' suspicions continued to be expressed with vigour, and by 1983 the general secretary of the NUT, Fred Jarvis, was convinced that the government was well on the way to controlling what was taught in schools. This, he insisted, was a dangerous development that 'contradicted the British tradition, which was to leave the curriculum to the teachers' (*The Times* 1983).

The Technical and Vocational Education Initiative (TVEI), launched in 1983, was widely taken as a major sign of the kind of policy change that justified such forebodings. It seemed to many to represent a major stage in the decline of teacher professionalism because it was announced with no prior consultation with educational interests and was even to be controlled not by the DES, but by the Manpower Services Commission which was responsible to the Department of Employment. One headteacher complained that it would mean that 'we would lose our professional prerogative to think or to plan and have to hand over our accountability to a body that was not accountable to the community' (Proud 1984; see also, e.g., McCulloch 1987). On the other hand, the TVEI did not simply follow the lines originally anticipated, but developed in unexpected ways that often appeared to enhance the roles of the teachers who were involved in the scheme. Janet Harland noted in relation to the TVEI what she called the 'central paradox' of

> the simultaneous emergence of two apparently or potentially conflicting features: on one hand, strong central control of a kind which has permitted the detailed intervention of a central government agency right down to the level of the classroom; and on the other a teacher response which is, in many of the pilot schemes, creative and innovative, and often indeed experimental and downright risky.          (Harland 1987, p. 39).

Harland described the teachers 'leading the TVEI crusade' as 'released prisoners'. These, however, were a 'very particular set of teachers', many of them drawn from the practical/technical/applied areas of the curriculum, who have 'in many schools led rather isolated and low-status professional lives' (Harland 1987, p. 47). On this view, teachers could interpret state policy in different ways, often leading it in directions unanticipated by its initiators (see also Helsby and McCulloch 1996).

Reinterpretations of the tradition of teacher professionalism also reflect the continuing role of this notion in the changing circumstances of the 1980s. In particular, the discourse developed by the British government in presenting and promoting its education reforms during this period placed an emphasis not on undermining or abandoning the tradition of teacher professionalism, but of reinterpreting it to meet new challenges. The government's emerging commitment to a National Curriculum and the conflicts to which this later gave rise encouraged specific discussion of the notion of teacher professionalism in a changed educational context. This was especially the case as the government's educational reforms also strongly emphasized the rights of parents as consumers, as against what were seen as the entrenched privileges of the 'producers': teachers, LEAs and the so-called 'educational Establishment'.

Sir Keith Joseph, as secretary of state for education between 1981 until 1986, was concerned to raise standards of pupil attainment, and in order to do so devised through the Inspectorate statements of what pupils in different subjects should be expected to achieve at particular age levels. On the other hand, he denied any intention of 'seeking to impose a centrally controlled curriculum, and to suppress the freedom to define the details of what is taught which had traditionally resided at local level' (Joseph 1984, p. 147). This reflected a continuing awareness of the strength of this tradition. Joseph attempted to articulate a changing relationship between local and national responsibilities, while still paying homage to teachers' established role in this area. Thus he stressed that 'the details of how subjects are taught will continue to be decided in each school, in the context of the local education authority's curricular policy', while at a national level there would be objectives for the range and balance of the curriculum, with defined levels of attainment to be reached at the ages of eleven and sixteen (Joseph 1984, p. 147). This was the general line that was maintained in the White Paper *Better Schools*, published in 1985, which also attempted an extended discussion of the nature of teachers' professionalism. It suggested that 'The professional work of the teacher includes the provision of information and the management of learning experiences: it also includes deciding how pupils should be grouped, the choice of teaching approaches and methods, and the choice of books, teaching materials and equipment.' Moreover, it added, 'This work extends to decisions about the advantages to be gained from introducing the applications of new technology across the curriculum, and from the involvement of people from outside the school – parents and employers, for example – in the educational process.' It concluded: 'These things may be seen as the means through which the curriculum is delivered: taken together, and combined with the attitudes and capabilities of the teacher, they also exercise a powerful influence on the curriculum' (DES 1985, p. 41). The idea of teacher professionalism in more general terms remained, however, somewhat ill-defined and amorphous in the policy documents of the 1980s, while the government remained unwilling to challenge the basic myth or tradition that continued to be associated with it.

During the development of the National Curriculum in 1987/8, the need to raise standards and to improve accountability was stressed even more strongly, but government statements continued to support a strong role for teachers. In particular, it was emphasized that teachers' control of pedagogy, or how to teach the curriculum, would remain unchallenged. For example, the consultation document on the National Curriculum, published in July 1987, noted that 'legislation should leave full scope for professional judgment and for schools to organise how the curriculum is delivered in the way best suited to the ages, circumstances, needs and abilities of the children in each classroom' (DES 1987, p. 11). Similarly, it was emphasized two years later that in translating the National Curriculum from policy into practice, the 'organisation of teaching and learning' should remain 'a professional matter for the head teacher and his or her staff' (DES 1989, para. 4.3). Moreover, the DES pointed out, 'What is specified will allow teachers considerable freedom in the way in which they teach, examples and materials used, selection of content and context, use of textbooks, etc. The legislation does not allow particular textbooks or teaching methods to be prescribed as part of a programme of study' (DES 1989, para. 4.15). In retrospect, such policy statements were drawing a distinction between the content of the school curriculum, which teachers would not be able to control, and the methods by which the curriculum would be delivered, which would remain within the domain of teachers. They were also willing to maintain at least some role for teachers in curriculum development. The relationship between the delivery and the assessment of the curriculum, meanwhile, remained unclear. Even so, despite these important adjustments, a notion of teacher professionalism as being related in a distinctive way to the curriculum domain was being preserved during this process. As Acker notes, the 'starting point' for innovations was recognized as 'a context where teachers' past autonomy in curricular matters was legendary', and it was a continuing awareness of this tradition that helped to shape and influence the policy process: 'The extent of curricular autonomy in the past explains why the non-statutory advice documents are so eager to list all the areas where prescription is *not* envisaged, in hopes of convincing teachers to "buy into" the reforms' (Acker 1990, pp. 270–1).

The secretary of state for education who was chiefly responsible for the introduction of the National Curriculum as part of the Education Reform Act of 1988, Kenneth Baker, also attempted to allay the concerns of 'some teachers' that the National Curriculum would 'prescribe how they go about their professional duties'. He insisted in ringing tones that 'We want to build upon the professionalism of the teacher in the classroom – the professionalism of the many fine and dedicated teachers throughout our education system' (*Hansard* 1987). It was not intended, he continued, 'to lay down how lessons should be taught, how timetables should be organised, or which textbooks should be used'. Indeed, according to Baker, the National Curriculum would provide ample 'scope for imaginative approaches developed by our teachers', such as in the TVEI and in the teaching of science in primary schools (*Hansard* 1987). On this account, the National Curriculum would provide a loose framework for teachers' work, to maintain and even enhance their autonomy in curriculum development. This was despite Baker's expressed determination to develop a National Curriculum that would embrace a full range of ten subjects (nine in primary schools) together with the requisite cross-curricular themes.

By contrast, the then prime minister, Margaret Thatcher, preferred to concentrate on the 'core' subjects, envisaging the establishment of a basic syllabus for English, mathematics and science, with simple tests for each. In her memoirs, she relates this preference explicitly to the need to reinterpret the established tradition of teachers' autonomy in a changing context. She acknowledges the existence of a strong tradition of teacher control in the curriculum area: 'The fact that since 1944 the only compulsory subject in the curriculum in Britain had been religious education reflected a healthy distrust of the state using central control of the syllabus as a means of propaganda' (Thatcher 1993, p. 590). At the same time, Thatcher maintains the view that the state should not try to 'regiment every detail of what happened in schools', and argues that the French 'centralised system' would 'not be acceptable in Britain' (p. 591). It is in this context that she seeks the retention of 'plenty of scope' for 'the individual teacher to concentrate with children on the particular aspects of the subject in which he or she felt a special enthusiasm or interest' (p. 593). Indeed, she emphasizes with the benefit of hindsight, 'I had no wish to put good teachers in a straitjacket' (p. 593). The established 'tradition' of the teacher in the curriculum domain is here strikingly acknowledged and treated as a starting point, to be encouraged and incorporated in current reforms as far as possible, and providing a criterion for the kinds of reforms that were seen as acceptable.

In spite of the official discourse which continued to avow an important place for teacher professionalism in the new order, many critics of the government's reforms feared that they signalled the abandonment of this tradition. The more general emphasis in the new education policies upon parental choice and the greater account-ability of schools suggested a hidden agenda in which the National Curriculum would effectively undermine the position of schoolteachers even in their most established domain. As Kenneth Baker's memoirs indicate, there were strong grounds for such fears. Despite his public affirmations of 'the professionalism of the teacher in the classroom', Baker later recalled that his preference for a 'full prescribed curriculum' had been partly in order to avoid schools being left 'adrift in a sea of fashionable opinions about what students should not, rather than should, be taught and at what age' (Baker 1993, p. 198). Moreover, he adds, 'Vagueness and lack of detail will allow an inadequate and lazy teacher to skip important parts' (p. 198). Here, a much more negative notion of the role of the teacher is reflected, as the National Curriculum is rationalized in terms of the need to limit teachers' influence in the classroom and to provide greater control over teachers themselves.

Opponents of the National Curriculum, alert to this prospect, therefore tended to assert the tradition of teacher professionalism in order to challenge the validity of the new reforms. Helen Simons, for example, emphasized what she called 'the professional role of the teacher and the loss to our education system of the pedagogical and curriculum developments that have taken place over the past twenty-five years' (Simons 1988, p. 78). She opposed the National Curriculum on the grounds that teachers would lose this professional role and become instead 'the implementers of curricula, judged nevertheless by the success of treatments they no longer devise' (p. 80). Similarly, Peter Gilroy warned that 'the professional autonomy of the teacher cannot long survive a situation where they have little or no control over the content of a curriculum which they are obliged by law to implement and test' (Gilroy 1991, p. 3).

These fears were heightened in the early 1990s as the implementation of the National Curriculum proved to be highly bureaucratic and intrusive in its effects. It was noted that teachers' 'professional knowledge' was 'at risk of becoming undermined by a heavily prescriptive, bureaucratic and managerial view of the curriculum, with an over emphasis on predetermined attainment targets and rigid forms of testing and assessment' (Ackland 1992, p. 88). There was evidence, moreover, that teachers themselves were conscious of losing their former role in this area. It was observed in 1993 that 'The two points on which the overwhelming majority of teachers agree are that the introduction of the curriculum has placed a heavy burden on their time, and that their professional concerns have been casually disdained' (*The Independent* 1993b). According to one history teacher, interviewed by Robert Phillips,

> My main objection to the concept of a National Curriculum is that it negates my professionalism and integrity as a teacher and a historian. The history course I have devised in my school works for me, my department and my pupils. It is one I can justify in breadth, scope, detail and balance. I am being asked to dismantle a syllabus I have faith and experience in, for one that is artificial, contrived and lacks integrity. Whereas I have always welcomed debate, suggestions and guidelines, I resent bitterly now having to teach someone else's package ... I am a qualified history teacher with ten years' teaching experience and as such feel more than capable of making my own decisions regarding the curriculum.                                                          (Phillips 1991, p. 22)

Phillips concluded: 'The State's new regulatory requirements have forced the history teacher to re-examine his/her role as autonomous curricular decision-maker' (p. 22).

At the same time, critics were also able to draw on the tradition of teacher professionalism either to suggest alternatives to the National Curriculum as it had been developed, or to argue for ways in which it might be maintained even in these unpromising circumstances. Philip O'Hear, for example, set out a case for 'a broader but less prescriptive curriculum based on overall aims, rather than the differently conceived content of 10 subjects, themselves chosen arbitrarily'. In such a model, he proposed, 'recognition of teachers' professionalism and knowledge of the learning needs and potential of their pupils would be given by allowing them a good deal of control of the control, order and delivery of the curriculum' (O'Hear 1994, p. 56; see also O'Hear and White 1991). Other critics recognized the deeply rooted 'professional ideology' of teachers, and suggested that this would continue to influence the teachers' notion of their role. According to one group of researchers, exploring the likely impact of the Education Reform Act at Key Stage 1,

> The passionately held commitment of most primary teachers in England and Wales to professional autonomy in both curriculum and pedagogy, the freedom of the individual school to decide how to educate its children, and the child-centred ideology which supports a pedagogy that aspires to be individualist, are all ideals that are held at the cost of a not inconsiderable sacrifice among English teachers.    (Broadfoot and Osborn 1988, p. 283)

On this view, teachers' own conception of their professionalism played a fundamental role in what teachers do at an everyday level, with the further implication that, 'If policy changes ride roughshod over such ideologies, and fail to take them into account, the result is likely to be widespread resentment, a lowering of morale, and with it, a reduced effectiveness' (Broadfoot and Osborn 1988, p. 283). On the other hand, as Ball and Bowe suggested, the 'whole notion of teacher professionalism' might still survive 'to provide a powerful critical vocabulary of aspects of the National Curriculum' (Ball and Bowe 1992, p. 108).

The continuing scope for contesting and reinterpreting the tradition of teacher professionalism in the domain of the curriculum was highlighted in the Dearing Review of the National Curriculum and its assessment. This followed a phase in which the demands of the National Curriculum were producing widespread protests among teachers, reaching a climax in 1993 when there was a widespread teachers' action to boycott tests for 7- and 14-year-olds (*The Independent* 1993b). Much of this agitation again revolved around notions of teacher professionalism, and the Dearing Review may be read as an initiative designed to reinterpret this tradition in a new way that would be more acceptable for teachers. The then education secretary, John Patten, was obliged to concede a distinctive professional role for teachers in curriculum organization, as it was confirmed in response to an enquiry from the National Union of Teachers (NUT) that 'Sir Ron [Dearing] and the Secretary of State are at one in maintaining that such questions are matters properly left to the professional judgment of teachers' (*TES* 1993). The Dearing Review proceeded to restate an explicit link between teacher professionalism and the school curriculum by recognizing that reducing the amount of prescriptive material in the National Curriculum would 'give more scope for professional judgement' (Dearing 1993, p. 17). In doing so, it made an important distinction between 'the essential matters, skills and processes which every school must by law teach' and 'the optional material which can be taught according to the professional judgement of teachers' (Dearing 1993, pp. 21–2). It remained to be seen whether this formula would provide the basis for lasting accommodation. At least initially it could be argued that the National Curriculum was 'back with the teachers' because the Dearing review had handed them back their 'professional responsibility', even if it might take time 'to get back into curriculum planning and the use of professional discretion without searching through the handbooks and directives for the right answer' (*TES* 1994c).

There remained many unresolved issues to be worked out following the publication of the Dearing Review and the new curriculum orders. Some critics continued to argue for greater scope for teacher autonomy with respect to different sectors of school education, for example through 'greater day-to-day control of their classroom and curriculum organisation' (Siraj-Blatchford 1994). Others questioned the major role assigned to external marking of examinations: 'To take the marking out of the hands of teachers may be a smart tactical move, and many may welcome the removal of the workload, but it also takes away a large measure of their professionalism and any hope that the tests might be put to constructive use' (*TES* 1994a). The general secretary of the NUT, Doug McAvoy, continued to voice strong opposition to the use of tests in primary schools, commenting: 'Our dispute has never been solely about workload. It is also about whether teachers perceive an encroachment on their professionalism' (*TES* 1994b). On the other hand, the Dearing Review provided those involved in developing the National Curriculum with a new opportunity to consolidate its role. For instance, Chris Woodhead, the then chief executive of the School Curriculum and Assessment Authority, could acknowledge that

> To have any effect, the words on the page of a national curriculum order need to be brought to life by teachers who have a confident grasp of the knowledge, understanding and skills encapsulated in each order, who are skilled classroom practitioners, and whose daily work brings real professional satisfaction.

If the 'overload' of the curriculum had 'undermined that satisfaction', he continued, the Dearing Review had now defined 'a significantly slimmer curriculum which will allow scope for the exercise of professional judgement' (Woodhead 1994; see also Tate 1994).

## CONCLUSIONS

Understanding teacher professionalism in terms of myth and tradition is a central means of beginning to address what and how teachers want to teach, no less than the ways in which teachers can respond to or initiate change. The socio-historical tradition of teacher autonomy in the curriculum domain continued to exert a strong influence on the kinds of reform that are permitted and sustained well into the 1980s and even the 1990s. For policy-makers, the existence of this tradition of teacher professionalism established parameters and expectations which defined the limits of desirable reform, and of expediency. For critics of policy in the 1980s and 1990s, it provided a potent resource, a continuing rebuke to contemporary changes and a symbol of alternative possibilities for changes yet to come. These differing connotations meant that the ideal of teacher professionalism deriving from the early post-war period was never moribund in the sense that it ceased to exert influence. On the contrary, it maintained a central role, contested fiercely as it was during a period of rapid policy innovations. The tensions that arose as a result may be read in terms of the contestation of this powerful historical myth, reflecting important differences about how to affirm, challenge and reinterpret teacher professionalism in a radically changing educational and political context.

*Chapter 3*

# The Politics of the Secret Garden

This chapter reflects on the limitations and constraints to teachers' supposed freedom that existed even in the 'Golden Age of teacher control (or non-control) of the curriculum' (Lawton 1980, p. 22). It also explores some of the changing political characteristics of the relationship between teachers and the school curriculum in England and Wales. During the earlier phase, the ideal of teacher autonomy was frequently belied by reality, but it was repeatedly endorsed among teacher groups and by a range of educational agencies as a central aspiration. In this situation, the integrity of teachers' roles in the school curriculum was constantly renegotiated in the face of current and impending threats. By focusing principally on the 1950s and 1960s, with the help of recently released documentary sources, it is possible to highlight the strength of the ideal of teacher autonomy in the curriculum domain, the inherent limitations and contradictions that were involved, and the efforts made to resolve the tensions that resulted.

Moreover, the role of the teacher in the curriculum domain has been viewed as a key source of their professionalism in England and Wales over the past fifty years. The incursions of the state and the introduction of the National Curriculum have been widely viewed as marking a major and unprecedented threat to this 'professionalism' (see e.g. Helsby and McCulloch 1996; McCulloch 1997a). Detailed historical research suggests that threats to teachers' professionalism were present throughout the post-war period, and that while the state was always held in suspicion for the control that it could potentially impose, it was also instrumental in helping to alleviate such threats.

## THE MINISTRY AND TEACHER FREEDOM

Historians who have emphasized the high degree of freedom enjoyed by teachers in the curriculum domain in the post-war period have argued that the Ministry of Education created the situation through its consistent refusal to intervene directly during these years. The focus of these arguments tends in practice to be on the curriculum of the secondary schools, but a more general case encompassing all teachers is commonly made. Lawton argues, for example (1980, p. 19), that after the Education Act of 1944, '*Laissez-faire* rather than rational planning prevailed and continued to be the curriculum philosophy for another twenty years.' According to Lawton, too (1980, p. 21), 'With the removal of the constraints of the Regulations after 1945 schools were free to embark upon any kind of secondary curriculum the teachers chose to offer.' Indeed, he suggests, 'A dangerous vacuum existed: the typical grammar-school curriculum changed very little in the post-war years; secondary-modern-school curricula, free of examination constraints, often lacked structure and purpose.' Thus, Lawton concludes (1980, p. 22), 'little thought was given to the curriculum, either locally or nationally'.

Chitty, in his account of central control of the school curriculum, follows a broadly similar line. He refers (1988, p. 326) to a 'cosy era of partnership and teacher autonomy' that in spite of apparent conflict in the early 1960s did not come under 'serious threat' until much later, especially following the changed economic circumstances of the mid-1970s. Simon also stresses (1991, p. 311) that 'the received (and official) view of the 1960s was that the curriculum (or what went on in schools) was the specific responsibility of the *teachers* – not of the local authorities (though their role here was unclear) and certainly not of the state – or the central government'. According to Simon (p. 319), 'any assessment of the 1960s must record this as a period of decisive change in terms of teacher professionalism, control, self-image, and even autonomy'. Above all, in Simon's view (*ibid.*), 'teachers were now seen as responsible for the curriculum – for what went on in schools'. The 1960s are therefore viewed as the 'heroic period' at least of secondary education in England and Wales, making gains that were later to be 'brought under control and curbed, whatever the cost' (*ibid.*).

As shown in the previous chapter, it is clearly true that during these years ideals of teacher freedom in the curriculum domain were uppermost, and that there was generally official approval for teacher control in this area. The ideal of teacher freedom was sometimes questioned and even criticized in official circles, but at least in principle it was generally upheld, often with a helpful detailed explanation of its wider implications. In early 1955, for example, the incoming minister of education, Sir David Eccles, sought to explore the frontiers of his authority. On this occasion, he asked his officials to explain to him the meaning of the maxims offered in the Ministry pamphlet *The New Secondary Education*, which had been published in 1947. In particular, he was interested in the curriculum of one of the three types of secondary school (grammar, technical and modern) that had developed in the new era of 'secondary education for all' since the Education Act of 1944 (see e.g. McCulloch 1994 for a general discussion of the distinctions between these schools and the pupils who attended them). He enquired whether this pamphlet was still in circulation, or whether it had been superseded, and continued,

> There is a passage which begins: 'The aim of the modern school is to provide a good all-round secondary education, not focussed primarily on the traditional subjects of the school curriculum etc.'. I do not know what this has come to mean i.e. what HMIs [Her Majesty's Inspectors] have told teachers it should mean. Unsystematic education? the children doing what they like best? or find easiest? How has this doctrine stood the test of experience?
>
> (Eccles 1955)

He also took the opportunity to pursue the further implications of this advice: 'The circular quoted above shows that M. of E. does give guidance about the curriculum, and one wonders how far this is pressed home by HMIs. It follows in greater or less degree that the notion that the Minister has nothing to do with the curriculum is an illusion' (*ibid.*). For example, he pointed out, the architect of the 1944 Education Act, R. A. Butler, had 'insisted' on religious education being taught in all schools; 'could I now insist, had I a mind so to do, on greater emphasis on English?' (*ibid.*). Eccles concluded, 'It is important when so many new secondary schools are to be built that the Minister should have a view. I do not want to dictate. But it is my duty to guide, and I should have to think very severely if you told me that "The New Secondary Education" still holds the field. And if it does not, what does?' (*ibid.*).

Eccles's officials hurried to clarify the situation. It was explained that the circular was now a little 'dated' but it was still being circulated and had not been withdrawn or superseded (Ministry of Education 1955). Religious education was specifically provided for under Section 25(2) of the 1944 Education Act, but, as was emphasized, 'No other subject is prescribed by statute, and the various bodies of Regulations governing the different types of educational establishment can say no more than that "The school shall be kept on a satisfactory level of efficiency."' (Ministry of Education 1955). Section 23 of the Act made the local education authorities responsible for the control of the secular instruction in county and voluntary schools in their area, other than aided secondary schools, and the governors responsible in aided secondary schools, 'save in so far as may be provided otherwise' by the rules of management or articles of government. Therefore,

> It follows that the Minister could not 'insist' on greater emphasis on English. But he can give guidance about the curriculum. Leaving aside the ordinary process of inspecting, and reporting on, individual schools, such guidance is given through the medium of Handbook of Suggestions – the very title is significant – and pamphlets on particular subjects, written by Her Majesty's Inspectors – again the title is significant. (Ministry of Education 1955)

Similar cautious testing of the possibilities that were available to the central authorities took place towards the end of the decade, this time with particular reference to the school science curriculum. As in other countries such as the United States, there was a great deal of political concern expressed at this time to ensure a supply of scientific manpower and a wider understanding of scientific and technological change, and this led to pressure being applied to 'modernize' the science curriculum in the schools (see, e.g., McCulloch *et al.* 1985; Waring 1979). Following the general election of 1959, a minister for science was appointed to stimulate new developments in this field. This minister, the experienced Conservative politician and former minister of education Lord Hailsham, wasted little time in raising key issues about curriculum reform. He argued (1959) in a letter to Sir David Eccles, who had retained his post as minister of education, that recent reports would tend to 'bring pressure to bear on us to improve still further both the quality and quantity of scientific and technical education'. For example, he suggested, there needed to be some attention given to the possibility of teaching science in primary schools. Moreover, he added,

> Whether primary schools can have a go at science teaching or not, I should have thought it worth a look to see whether the approach to science teaching could not be a little more via simple engines and mechanisms, even at a very early age, and less as now either by way of the birds and bees or by way of what are fundamentally the more academic subjects of elementary physics and chemistry. (1959)

This initiative was rewarded by a flurry of high-level discussion (Ministry of Education 1960a).

Lord Hailsham's next salvo was met with sterner resistance from officials at the Ministry of Education who were increasingly anxious about the potential threat that the minister for science represented for the ideal of teacher freedom. At the beginning of 1961, Hailsham wrote again to Eccles to propose a major new initiative in the curriculum. This would involve developing textbooks for use in key areas of the curriculum: 'The question I wish to raise is whether we cannot do more than we are doing to commission and create first class textbooks in the English language and to define curricula to which such text books should conform.' These would include 'elementary subjects such as reading', advanced subjects, and 'manuals of instruction in teaching methods such as are used in training colleges' (Hailsham 1961). He was aware of the likely objections that would be made to this suggestion, but sought to reconcile his idea with the usual emphasis on teacher freedom as he continued:

> Of course I realise and respect the traditional view held here that the content of the curriculum and text books should not be a matter for the Ministry. But this surely only means, if the need for better text books is accepted, the creation of machinery outside the Ministry for enquiring into the need and filling any gaps there may be?          (*ibid.*)

This kind of device, he urged, would help to prune the curriculum of 'unwanted lumber'. A further advantage in Hailsham's view would be that 'we would capture an international market of great value to us, both commercially and spiritually, and that we could exploit still further, in the fields of Asia and Africa particularly, the currency of the English language'. It would at the same time address what he saw as the 'broader question' of 'whether, and how, modernisation of school science curricula can be brought about'. A charitable trust such as the Nuffield Foundation might well be 'better qualified' than the government to 'spark something off' (*ibid.*), and so he was also happy to encourage the development of what was to be launched, the following year, as the Nuffield Foundation Science Teaching Project.

On this occasion, officials at the Ministry of Education were quick to signal their strong misgivings. Toby Weaver, in particular, observed caustically that

> Of the many baffling aspects of the English educational system, the one that is most likely to cause acute impatience to a man of action like Lord Hailsham is the process by which the curriculum of the schools is determined. When the curriculum is criticised he is moved to take it by the scruff of the neck in the belief that he can shake sense into it.   (Weaver 1961)

However, Weaver insisted, 'I do not believe that strong arm tactics are likely to be in the least effective or that there is any alternative to the patient working out of syllabuses by teachers' (*ibid.*). This, he explained, was because

> In our system there is no centre of power where differences can be resolved. In practice each science teacher bases his syllabus on a mixture of his own experience, the known views of the professional associations and of H.M. Inspectorate, and the examination syllabus chosen by the school. The points of change and growth are therefore likely to be found in the Science Panel of H.M. Inspectorate, in the Science Masters' Association, and in the Subject Panels of the several University examining bodies which in turn are subject to the influence of the SSEC [Secondary Schools Examination Council]. It is not clear how this process is likely to be improved or accelerated by the intervention of outsiders, however powerful or distinguished.          (*ibid.*)

He accepted that a meeting might be held on the topic, but hoped that this would lead to a 'better understanding' of 'the limitations of such action', and he was anxious that textbooks should constitute only a 'peripheral subject': 'the idea that Ministers should commission or otherwise bring textbooks into existence makes me shudder' (*ibid.*).

These views were supported by other officials at the Ministry of Education. Dame Mary Smieton, permanent secretary at the Ministry, was prepared to countenance 'outside general enthusiasm on the part of eminent scientists', but she continued to emphasize 'the patient practical work of revising syllabuses and working out new teaching methods which can only be done by those who are close to the task' (Smieton 1961). R. A. R. Tricker, senior inspector for science, was also resolute in his conviction (Ministry of Education 1961a) that 'in this country it was not possible to dictate the syllabus from the centre'. It therefore appears that in spite of some temptation to the contrary on the part of ministers, and a deep-seated suspicion of central authority that was often shown by representatives of teachers and local education authorities, the state was in general not inclined to assert its own control in the area of the school curriculum during these years.

A greater danger to the ideal of teacher freedom lay elsewhere, in the influence exerted by public examinations and the examination boards. Hopes were often emphasized during the years of the Second World War that examinations would come to play a less important role in the curriculum. Sir Cyril Norwood, chairman of the SSEC, argued that the status of the teaching profession would not be raised 'until the teachers were given more responsibility and made to face up to it'. According to Norwood, the nature of examinations was central to this development: 'At present teachers taught to an Examination standard which was set by an outside Examining Body. Teachers should themselves be able to work out a scheme of education and to assess it.' If teachers could be trained to accept responsibility in this area, Norwood concluded, 'they might in time become a self-governing profession and be esteemed as such' (Norwood 1942a). On the other hand, 'So long as they accept external control as to what they shall teach and external assessment of the way in which they have taught, they can never rise above the rank of journeyman.' Thus, 'Just as the Universities must be free to conduct their own teaching and research within their own domain, so must the school teachers be free in theirs' (Norwood 1942b). However, the examining boards insisted on maintaining control over examinations, and it also became evident that teachers, headteachers and subject associations were in many cases unwilling to take on this increased responsibility. Accountability to outside expertise and to the wider public was cited as an important reason for retaining external examinations at this time (see also McCulloch 1994, esp. ch. 7).

By the 1950s, the role of the examining boards had increased, especially in relation to the nature of the secondary school curriculum, but also at other levels. This in turn tended to reduce the freedom of the teachers themselves. The significance of examinations can be seen first by tracing their effect on one type of school that was initially intended to be entirely outside their influence, the secondary modern schools. They were also central to the controversy that led to the setting up in 1964 of the Schools Council for the Curriculum and Examinations.

## THE CASE OF THE SECONDARY MODERN SCHOOLS

In the system of secondary education that developed following the Second World War, secondary modern schools were designed to cater for the majority of pupils who were not selected at the age of eleven to go to grammar school or to a technical school. They were also intended to avoid the use of formal examinations in order to encourage the development of new kinds of curriculum and teaching methods that would be appropriate for the pupils who attended them. This concern had been evident since the 1920s, when the Hadow Report on the education of the adolescent had emphasized (Board of Education 1926, p. 150) that although their courses should lead towards a 'definite objective', they 'need not be influenced to the same extent by the requirements of an external examination'. It was envisaged that this would give teachers in such schools greater freedom to frame courses in the different subjects than was available in the existing secondary schools which were oriented towards examinations.

In the 1940s, when the secondary modern schools were introduced, there were determined efforts to maintain this approach. The Ministry of Education emphasized (1945, p. 21) that these schools should remain free from the 'pressures' of external examinations, and that this 'invaluable freedom' should help them to 'advance along the lines they themselves feel to be right'. This view was supported by many local education authorities. In Lancashire, the largest LEA outside London, the chief education officer, A. L. Binns, set out to follow the lead set by the Ministry. He insisted (1946) that the teachers and headteachers of the secondary modern schools should assume major responsibilities in their development, and that they should be allowed 'a very wide measure of freedom to experiment', especially with regard to the curriculum. In particular, he argued, the secondary modern school curriculum should not be allowed to become 'a reflection of the Grammar School' which 'could only be a pale one', whereas 'the Modern School can, I am sure, achieve remarkable success by striking out on entirely different lines in its curriculum, while adopting all that is best in the Grammar School and Public School conception of a complete education'. At the same time, Binns counselled the secondary modern schools against the 'temptation' of using or developing external examinations, which would shape and restrict the curriculum (Binns 1946). In the same vein, Stewart Mason, director of education in Leicestershire, hoped (1946) that external examinations would not be allowed to 'creep into' the secondary modern schools: 'As such they have only started and we certainly don't want an exam to cabin them before we even know in what direction they will find themselves going.' In this regard, Mason noted, they would need to resist the demands of many parents, 'who will want a piece of paper of more than local currency for their children to show employers', and of many teachers and headteachers 'who welcome an external exam as giving their pupils "something to work for", and also as providing a readymade standard of efficiency' (Mason 1946).

By the 1950s, it had become clear that that such demands could not easily be resisted. It was increasingly argued that the secondary modern schools should be encouraged to enter their pupils into external examinations, especially the General Certificate of Education (GCE) examinations that were associated with the grammar schools. HMIs pondered whether the GCE might be a legitimate goal for such schools, and agreed (Ministry of Education 1956) that 'both staff and pupils might benefit from such a stimulus'. On the other hand, there continued to be an emphasis on flexibility, based on considerations of the nature of local communities, parental demands, local industrial demands, and the qualities of the teachers and headteachers. One leading Ministry official, M. P. Roseveare, argued strongly (1955) that 'teachers must be given, and helped to exercise, full academic freedom, i.e. freedom to determine what and how and when and at what pace progress is best for the pupil and is possible for the teachers'. According to Roseveare, examining, stocktaking, and checking effectiveness and progress were 'undoubtedly proper functions in teaching', and should be 'a normal and regular internal operation in any school'. On the other hand, he warned, '*External* examinations inevitably restrict the teacher's freedom; he must to some extent relate his teaching to the exam. syllabus' (Roseveare 1955). Geoffrey Lloyd as minister of education (1958) also continued to resist 'any developments that would, in the result, endanger the freedom of the Heads and their staffs to devise their own curricula and teaching methods or impose on them a uniformity of aim or method'.

In spite of the opposition of the Ministry of Education, the Secondary Schools Examinations Council was keen to develop a new form of examination that would be suitable for pupils at the secondary modern schools. The SSEC established a committee chaired by Robert Beloe, chief education officer for Surrey, to consider the issue, but there remained a great deal of opposition to the idea partly because it represented an encroachment into the ideal of teacher freedom. For example, S. T. Broad, chief education officer for Hertfordshire, made a 'plea' (1959) that 'this question is fundamentally and essentially a *professional* matter', in that the teacher 'should not have to be looking over his shoulder at the "employer" or the "public", wondering what such uninformed people are going to commit him to' (Broad 1959). Nevertheless, Beloe's committee proposed a new examination which eventually resulted in the establishment of the Certificate of Secondary Education (CSE) (SSEC 1960). This created widespread suspicion about the likely implications for the secondary modern schools and for teachers. Some, like J. M. Pullan in Bristol, objected (1962) to the increasing prominence of examinations which seemed to be 'rapidly taking a stranglehold on the whole educational system'.

The CSE examination that was developed did incorporate a central role for teachers. The SSEC science panel, for instance, welcomed (1962) the emphasis given to 'the control of this examination being placed largely in the hands of the teachers in the schools concerned', and approved the fact that 'the proposed regulations will enable a school to submit its own syllabus for examination and that it may organise (under external assessment) its own marking'. Indeed, it concluded, 'These opportunities will give the scope to which enterprising and progressive teachers are entitled and should be preserved even though they may not be used to any great extent at present' (SSEC 1962). It continued to be emphasized that the Ministry of Education and examination boards comprised 'the framework within which the teacher could exercise his responsibility in as professional a way as possible and there could be close integration of teaching and examining roles' (Morrell 1964). There remained, even so, major differences for example over whether a 'common core' should be introduced which critics such as Gordon Bessey, the director of education in Cumberland, viewed (1964) as 'an incursion into the syllabus arrangements and direction of individual schools'. L. W. Norwood, joint secretary of the SSEC, was alert (1964) to the basic issue that was underlying this question: 'What is a school based examination or quis custodiet ipsos custodes?'. However, he insisted that in spite of the view expressed by Bessey and others that 'any school can be a law unto itself in the matter of syllabus content and examining techniques whilst conceding to the Board the right to withhold a certificate as a result of moderation', it was within the powers of any regional board 'to *require* candidates in some or indeed all schools to take a common core paper as part of the examination' (Norwood 1964). Derek Morrell at the Ministry of Education was sympathetic to Norwood's view, but also suggested (1964) that it might not be necessary to insist on such devices because the existence of the examination itself created 'pressures on the teacher to conform', that were 'far stronger than the pressures, or the individual urge, to innovate'. At the same time, Morrell floated a further question as to the potential role of the Ministry when he asked, 'granted that most teachers will, at any given moment in time, adopt a common-core of content more or less in line with the consensus of professional opinion, how far is it necessary to control those who, for both good and bad reasons, do not?' (Morrell 1964). This was an issue that raised implications too troubling to pursue further, and it was generally agreed that further administrative regulations were not appropriate. As the senior inspector J. J. Withrington argued, 'the cure is worse than the disease. Perfect moderation casteth out life ... . There will be powerful enough forces tending to produce uniformity in my view. We do not need to add to them by administrative action right at the start' (Withrington 1964a).

The increasing importance of external examinations in the secondary modern schools was highly significant in helping to undermine the relative freedom and autonomy that had initially been ascribed to them, and in particular to the teachers in the schools. Despite the clear misgivings of the Ministry of Education, the SSEC overrode the ideal of teacher freedom to encourage the further growth of examinations in the secondary modern schools. More broadly, these developments were symptomatic of a wider trend towards an emphasis on examinations that seemed to many to negate the principle of teacher freedom and of professionalism itself.


## A CRISIS OF TEACHER PROFESSIONALISM?

The increasing influence of external examinations was again strongly emphasized in the early 1960s during the negotiations that led in 1964 to the establishment of the Schools Council for the Curriculum and Examinations. It was widely acknowledged at this time that the principles of teacher freedom in the curriculum were being endangered by the influence of examinations, and that urgent action was necessary in order to reassert them. The Ministry of Education supported this view to such an extent that it warned that the professionalism of teachers was itself at risk, especially in the secondary schools.

The basic problem was well articulated in April 1960 in a response by the Ministry of Education to discussions over the revision of the school science curriculum. On the one hand, it noted,

> It is a basic principle of the English educational system that schools are free to decide their own curriculum and that there is no central direction. This sets strict limits to what can be achieved by any outside body seeking to influence curricula in science as in other fields, since any arrangement or proposal which could be shown directly to contravene the principle would be unacceptable to the schools.                    (Ministry of Education 1960b)

In practice, however, it recognized 'various ways' by which 'those responsible for shaping the curriculum in the schools can be and are influenced'. In the secondary schools, and especially in grammar schools, it identified in particular the influence of external examinations such as the GCE and the university open scholarship examinations, 'since the examination syllabuses largely determine the lines on which individual subjects are taught' (*ibid.*).

These concerns came to the fore as the Ministry became increasingly involved in efforts to revise the school curriculum. In March 1962, it established a Curriculum Study Group based in the Ministry, a development that was widely criticized as being likely to lead to increased central control over the curriculum. The *TES*, for example, noted that

> Until this week it was often a matter for boasting that in this country, unlike others, the Minister of Education had no say in the curriculum. It was held to be one of the pillars of our freedom. No one inquired particularly why this English convention was so much better than the system in France, which anyhow was the homeland of liberty, equality and the rest of it . . . . That, however, is all now in the past. (*TES* 1962a)

A working party was set up under Sir John Lockwood to consider a more acceptable arrangement, and a more insidious influence was identified in the form of examinations. The National Union of Teachers, for example, acknowledged the need for new approaches as it accepted (Powell-Davies 1963) that 'the schools are becoming increasingly the objects of external pressures which are none the less real because they act indirectly through such means as external examinations, the entry requirements of higher education institutions and the professions, and the new technological environment in which the schools have to function'. Moreover, it added, 'We agree that in such a sociological context there is real danger that the autonomy of the school and the freedom of the teacher could become increasingly meaningless' (Powell-Davies 1963).

The minister of education, Sir Edward Boyle, argued the case for a representative Schools Council in terms that emphasized the existing threat to teacher freedom in the curriculum domain. He explicitly endorsed the principle of teacher freedom and stressed that a new Schools Council would help to uphold it. According to Boyle (1963), it had 'long been public policy in England and Wales to regard the schools curriculum and teaching methods as exclusively the concern of the teachers', so that 'In theory, the teachers are free to decide for themselves what they want to teach, and how they want to teach it.' In practice, however, 'the teacher's freedom in curricular matters has been increasingly curtailed by external examinations, and by other external influences on the curriculum'. Indeed, Boyle noted,

> Only the nursery and infants' schools escape these pressures. At all other stages of the educational process, public examinations, the entry requirements of professional bodies, selection tests for entry to the grammar schools, and other influences besides, shape curriculum, teaching methods and school organisation in degrees varying from almost complete domination to a strong indirect influence. (Boyle 1963)

Ministry officials elaborated on this view in their evidence to the working party, as they proposed what they called (Ministry of Education 1963a) a 'consortium' to provide a forum for studying common problems.

Another long memorandum produced by the Ministry of Education to discuss what it called 'The outlines of the problem' (Ministry of Education 1963b) similarly disavowed any intention of seizing control over the school curriculum, but warned in trenchant tones of the dangers posed by public examinations. It acknowledged that to the 'maximum possible extent', every school should be 'free to adopt a curriculum and teaching methods based on its own needs and evolved by its own staff'. What was at issue, it suggested, was 'the contemporary interpretation of the policy, not the policy itself'. This was because the policy was 'in danger'. It had been interpreted too negatively, and needed to be 'restored to full efficacy' through cooperative action. The Ministry argued that current practice recognized 'the right of the schools to take *particular* curricular decisions within a framework of general determinants, or norms, formulated as an expression of the community's interest in the *general* character of the educational process' (*ibid.*). However, the line between the 'particular' and the 'general' was in its view moving in the wrong direction, and the scope for particular curricular decisions on the part of the schools was becoming smaller:

> The formulation of norms is tending to pass out of the hands of those to whom the community has entrusted this responsibility, and those responsible for taking particular decisions (namely, the teachers) are not being enabled to play a sufficient part in the processes of formulating the norms which constitute the general framework for their work.
>
> (*ibid.*)

In the view of the Ministry, the influence of public examinations was largely responsible for this problem. For example,

> In the case of the grammar schools, the norms which the schools have to observe have invaded the area of the particular to such an extent that there is today little reality in the concept of the school as the basic unit of educational reform, with its curriculum based on its own needs and evolved by its own staff. And this invasion has simply happened: no one has willed it: no one desires it. External examinations have moved in, and now dominate the curriculum more firmly than ever before. To a wholly undesirable extent, the teachers have to teach what someone else has decided to examine.   (*ibid.*)

The secondary modern schools and the junior schools were moving in the same direction, it argued, so that it was only the early stages of primary education that remained 'almost wholly free to take the full range of curricular decisions proper to the schools, within norms which press only lightly on their work'. By contrast, the sixth form curriculum in the secondary schools 'has so far passed into the hands of the examining boards as to constitute an effective transfer of responsibility for the establishment of many important norms, as well as a transfer of responsibility for the particular curricular decisions that are proper to the schools'. The Ministry concluded that the examining boards had assumed such control, and examinations had gained such influence, because there was no 'standing machinery' that was adequate to regulate or reverse 'trends that have long been recognised as dangerous'. It was to provide such a means of regulation, through cooperation on the basis of a 'consortium' arrangement, that it was necessary to establish the Schools Council.

According to the Ministry, therefore, the accelerating trend towards competitive examinations at all levels of the education system was the root cause of the increasing threat to the ideal of teacher freedom in the curriculum. The popularity of examinations, moreover, had broad social causes rather than being based on educational principles or even on 'empire building' by the examination boards which after all, the Ministry conceded, had 'only done their job'. It was the nature of social demand that was fundamentally responsible in the form of trends such as 'society's need for more and more better educated citizens and workers, the desire of parents and pupils to respond to this need, and the consequent demand for specific evidence of educational achievement' (Ministry of Education 1963b). In other words, it was what Michael Young (1958) had satirically described as the 'rise of the meritocracy' that posed the principal danger to the ideal of teacher freedom in these years.

## CONSTRAINTS ON CURRICULUM REFORM

The tensions around examinations and the establishment of the Schools Council served to highlight the practical limitations of teacher freedom in the curriculum domain. These continued to be demonstrated, as the 1960s progressed, through the unexpected problems that were encountered by initiatives to reform the school curriculum. Such initiatives were frequently unsuccessful due to a range of constraints that tended to discourage teachers from promoting curriculum change.

The importance of curriculum reform in the interests of social progress and economic competitiveness was an increasingly strong theme in the early 1960s. School science reform designed to allow more effective competition with the United States and the Soviet Union was a common demand. Secondary schools, however, seemed generally ill equipped to satisfy such calls, especially because no single agency appeared to have the authority that was necessary to sanction or pursue curriculum reform on a national basis. This problem was observed with some shrewdness by the *TES*:

> The curriculum of the secondary school is like last week's disastrous Derby. Too many subjects jostle for position. Not all of them are of undisputed value. Not all of them will stay the course. Out at front, at least at the start, are one or two, such as English and mathematics, which hold their place by tradition or plain utility. Struggling behind are some others, such as art and music, which many people advance but not so many are prepared to back. In between are a cosmopolitan bunch, including the foreign languages, which can only get ahead if they push the others out of the way. Educationists, like the stewards, may deplore the situation; but nobody has a clear idea of what should be done to prevent it. (*TES* 1962b)

The *TES* attributed this difficulty partly to the limitations of the timetable, but also to what it called 'a tradition, in many ways admirable, of liberty in our schools'. It recognized that the schools had tried to respond to changing national needs, but pointed out the increasing pressure both for a trained community to maintain and improve the standard of living, and for education for economic planning. It warned, therefore, that 'If this is so and if it is public money that is to be invested, the temptation may well grow on future governments to replace persuasion by compulsion, to modify the freedom of the schools so that they fit an overall plan' (*TES* 1962b). It was at least in part to avoid this prospect that a number of initiatives were developed to support the role of teachers.

In the early 1960s, since no effective mechanism appeared to exist for promoting curriculum change on a national basis, the potential role of individual teachers was often emphasized. The problem with this, as was recognized, was that it was difficult to pass on what was successful in one school with one teacher or group of teachers to other schools with different teachers and their own sets of problems. As the senior inspector

J. J. Withrington observed with respect to attempts to improve the 'relevance' of the school curriculum, 'In fact there has been a very great deal of experiment with new subject matter over the past 40 years and in this sense experiment is going on all the time' (Withrington 1964a). Much that was learned in this process, according to Withrington, 'stays with the originator or dies when he goes on to higher places'. Some nevertheless, he added, 'seeps gradually into the practice of the teaching profession as a whole' (Withrington 1964a). Overall this seemed too haphazard and too gradual a process upon which to depend, and the view gained ground that teachers required outside assistance in order to make the most of their 'experiments'.

One promising line of development was through the Nuffield Foundation, a charitable trust with a tradition of 'filling the gaps in Government planning' (*The Observer* 1962). In April 1962, the minister of education was able to announce that the Foundation was investing a quarter of a million pounds in a long-term development programme for school science education. This followed long discussions with the science teachers' associations, the Science Masters' Association and the Association of Women Science Teachers, which had been examining possibilities for new science syllabuses since the later 1950s (see McCulloch *et al.* 1985, esp. chs 5, 7). The Foundation was well aware that 'in the intricate and tangled pattern of organization which constitutes the English school system', it was 'extremely difficult to determine where the main responsibility for curriculum development lies' (Nuffield Foundation 1964). In principle, as the Foundation saw, the content of school curricula was the responsibility of individual schools, but in practice for grammar schools, with which it was mainly concerned, the curriculum followed the examinations, and the examinations were under the ultimate control of the SSEC.

The Foundation benefited from a close but informal working relationship with the science teaching associations on the one hand, and the Ministry of Education on the other. Nuffield officials gave generous acknowledgement to the 'pioneering efforts' of the science teachers in order to avoid challenging the established precept of teacher autonomy. While maintaining its independence of the Ministry, it also gained unofficial advice and support for its initiative from Ministry officials and the Curriculum Study Group. The CSG was therefore able to claim that practising teachers were themselves responsible for the curriculum innovations that were being introduced: 'This work is *professionally* controlled neither by the CSG nor the Nuffield Foundation: it is being carried out as a completely independent professional exercise by the teachers concerned' (Curriculum Study Group 1963). Moreover, it added with some enthusiasm,

> This is likely to lead in the fairly near future to proposals for related, but more broadly aimed, projects in both science and mathematics designed, like the initial projects, to give practising teachers the opportunity to work full time on the advancement of their professional skills, through the development of ideas already being tried out in a limited way in the schools.                    (*ibid.*)

This would give teachers more opportunity to carry out development work of their own, it was affirmed, while also effectively confining the CSG to a support and advisory role:

> just as the work of HMI in the schools stops far short of official control or direction, so the work of the CSG in this more generalised context involves no infringement of the right of the teachers to take their own professional decisions, whether they are working within a development team or considering using the results of such work in the schools.    (*ibid.*)

Not all were convinced by such disavowals, but they preserved the official line of teachers' professional autonomy while allowing scope for active and systematic support for curriculum reform.

Nevertheless, it remained clear that the wide range of interests and pressures on the school curriculum were both undermining the autonomy of teachers and making it more difficult to pursue curriculum reform with any degree of consistency or vigour. The review of the curriculum and examinations conducted by Sir John Lockwood's working party in 1963–4 (Ministry of Education 1963c) raised the key issue of how far 'general determinants' should constrain schools and teachers in the curriculum field:

> How much influence is in fact exerted by external determinants and how far is this influence in excess of what can legitimately be allowed? Ultimate and complete freedom for each school is impossible and indeed an incomprehensible concept. But it is widely felt that external pressures on the curriculum have now become excessive and the encroachments on the due liberty of schools objectionable.

It identified a large number of 'sources of pressure'. The first was the Ministry itself. Although as a direct source of pressure 'the Ministry's hand rests lightly on the schools' curriculum', there were also indirect pressures 'of some force' that could be exerted by inspectors and through decisions over buildings and facilities. Second, local education authorities sometimes took 'too literally' their statutory rights over the curriculum in order to 'exercise too direct a control'. Hence, as was observed,

> The proposal to teach, say, French in a primary school may have to be referred to the LEA not merely in order to get necessary staff but to gain approval for the project as an educational idea. A local authority may dictate curricular policy by refusing to permit the appointment of the necessary staff ... decisions about buildings and their equipment or over the amount of money available for libraries and textbooks may have a powerful effect on what the schools actually can do. (Ministry of Education 1963c)

The third was the now familiar role of the public examination system. Fourth, the demands made by universities and training colleges tended in some cases to distort the school curriculum. It was its potential capacity to explore and address this wide range of influences that made the new Schools Council so attractive.

In practice, however, the Schools Council was often unable to redress the balance in favour of teacher autonomy. Several of the major curriculum development projects established by the Schools Council found themselves virtually helpless to promote curriculum reform of a fundamental kind. One of the least successful, Project Technology, was so frustrated in its aims that it sent a questionnaire to teachers who were taking part to find out what was inhibiting them. This produced a wide range of 'inhibiting influences' that tended to discourage teachers from introducing some form of technological activities. First was external recognition in the form of examinations and the requirements of universities, colleges and employers. Second was school organization, comprising time allowances, timetable flexibility and sizes of classes. Third was physical provision, accommodation or equipment. Fourth was finance or the method of financing. Finally, the teachers consulted in this questionnaire pointed to personal issues such as training and background, and a shortage of fresh ideas (Harrison 1968). The director of the project, Geoffrey Harrison, suggested that 'the pressures of the examinations themselves (with all the associated vested interests of text-book publishers and apparatus manufacturers)' was the main single inhibiting factor, followed by the attitudes, training and experience of the teachers themselves (*ibid.*). At the same time, he acknowledged the interrelated nature of such factors, and argued that 'it is difficult to get at the root causes of these pressures and to allow more fundamental needs to take effect' (*ibid.*).

The practical and everyday constraints on teachers that were indicated in such projects are also evident in some empirical studies of teachers' classroom management published in the 1960s and 1970s. For example, Philip Taylor, himself a leading supporter of teachers' control and autonomy, found in his discussions with teachers in secondary schools, in the three subject areas of English, science and geography, a wide range of ambitions and experiences:

> One discussion began with the confident assertion that you began planning a course by determining its aims; another with the very tentative comment: 'Much depends on the qualifications and interests of the teachers', and yet a third with the statement: 'We are, of course, creatures of our environment and not free to choose. There are such things as examinations and syllabuses.'                                              (Taylor 1970, p. 9)

In these discussions, it was the practical constraints on teachers' planning of courses that appeared to be uppermost in many cases, rather than the freedom and autonomy of the received ideal.

A later example of similar research, published in the 1980s (Calderhead 1984), commented on how the curriculum innovations of the 1960s and 1970s had generally developed outside the schools, but had often not been successfully implemented in the classroom, or else had not operated there as had originally been intended. At the same time, it emphasized the practical limitations that tended to impinge on the teacher in terms of managing the curriculum:

> Decisions about what ought to be taught and how are value judgements which are made by people and agencies both within and beyond the school, and such decisions obviously influence how teachers plan and teach. The recommendations of HMIs, the curriculum guidelines of LEAs, externally set examinations and policy decisions within the school may all contribute to the syllabus that a teacher is expected to follow and the materials that are made available                                              (Calderhead 1984, pp. 82–3).

The views of colleagues, parents and others would also have a major influence over the practices of teachers. The strongly held views of one secondary school mathematics teacher, for example, 'obviously did not persuade his head of department, headteacher or for that matter some of the parents, all of whom possessed quite different, more traditional conceptions of schoolwork', and the overall result was that 'Together they made it quite clear that he would rapidly have to change his ideas' (*ibid.*, p. 83).


CONCLUSIONS

The Ministry's protestations of innocence, its constant avowals of support for the principle of teacher freedom in the curriculum, need not be taken totally at face value. Teachers and local education authorities were always suspicious of increased central control, and indeed there were some indications of incipient interest in this area, following the lead taken by other countries. In 1961, for example, the Inspectorate's secondary education panel discussed ideas raised at a recent conference held in Sweden on the subject of 'Ability and educational opportunity in a modern economy'. A 'general discussion' followed on 'the relative merits of a system of laissez faire and of greater central direction' (Ministry of Education 1961b), and it was agreed that all would depend on 'the benevolence and enlightenment of the directing administrators'. Four years later, following a presentation by a Japanese delegation on the prescribed use of textbooks, it was suggested (DES 1965) that the 'attitude towards central planning of the curriculum' needed to be considered further: 'We have, on the whole, worked on the principle of freedom for schools to plan their own curricula; but, in fact, public examinations prescribed syllabuses to a considerable extent. There was currently some tendency to doubt the wisdom of entire freedom, and the School Council's work was tending to draw curricula together'. These were stirrings that, as Chitty and others have suggested, became a decisive theme a decade later in the context of economic and industrial decline.

In the 1950s and 1960s, on the other hand, a more potent and at the same a more insidious threat existed in the shape of the competitive pressures surrounding examinations. The expansionism and economic growth that largely characterized these years engendered social and economic influences that effectively contradicted the ideal of teacher freedom. They helped to undermine the distinctive principles of the secondary modern schools, and more generally asserted a role, as Boyle put it, 'varying from almost complete domination to a strong indirect influence'. In the light of these competing pressures, it is important to reassess the characteristics of the 'secret garden' of the school curriculum before the introduction of the National Curriculum, and the nature of the many different initiatives that were developed over these years. While the ideal of teacher autonomy in the curriculum domain and the notion of teacher professionalism that derived from it were virtually sacrosanct in these years, the practice was fiercely contested in a number of different arenas. The surface equanimity was belied by the strong undercurrents below.

# Chapter 4

# Memories of a Golden Age

Teachers' enduring memories of what is often regarded as a 'golden age' of teaching before the National Curriculum and the educational reforms of the 1990s provide a further means of engaging with the politics of professionalism in its longer-term framework of development. The interviews conducted with secondary school teachers and policy informants for the PCT study in the 1990s highlight a widely held view that the National Curriculum had ushered in a radically new phase that contrasted vividly with the situation that had existed in the 1960s, 1970s and 1980s. This memory was contested in that while many teachers lamented the loss of professional freedom associated with this earlier period, at least some others were enthusiastic about the change. These differences are highly significant as they provide a basis for opposing views in assessing the role of the teacher in secondary schools in the 1990s, between those who complain about the reduced opportunities to control what they teach and how they teach it, and those who perceive new possibilities emerging from this general development.

At first sight it may appear that only teachers with personal experience of teaching before the introduction of the National Curriculum in 1988 would have memories of the *ancien régime*. Those trained under the strictures of the National Curriculum, with no experience of earlier expectations or approaches, might be expected to have no memories of the 'secret garden'. This indeed is the view that emerges in one published account written by a new teacher, Rosemary Chapman:

> Teaching to the National Curriculum has caused few problems. I have not had to adapt my approach to conform to the requirements of the National Curriculum as has been the case for experienced colleagues, because I have known nothing else. It has been there since my first year in college and my first year of teaching. It has provided me with a supportive framework within which to work. I have not felt overloaded by the curriculum, but as my children are four and five year olds, my experience must be very different from that of teachers of more senior classes. They are having to cope with complex procedures and tend to have a much more prescriptive timetable. As I become more experienced, I may come to resent what my colleagues see as unacceptable government control of the curriculum, but I have no past as a teacher and so I do not see my professionalism being challenged.
>
> (Chapman 1995, p. 38)

However, the presence and effects of teachers' memories are more complex than this view would suggest. Memories may be drawn from childhood or one's own schooling as well as from direct teaching experience, and may also be shaped by the reminiscences of family members, or teaching colleagues, or other acquaintances. It is from a wide range of such sources that we may begin to construct the nature of teachers' professional memory.

## THE POLITICS OF MEMORY

Earlier work on memory tended to emphasize its individual, psychological characteristics. Over the past decade, it is the social construction of memory that has been among the most important aspects to have been developed. The connections between 'memory' and 'history', that is, between individualized perceptions of a personal past and a more generalized public record of the past, provide a further key issue. The significance of memory as a means of understanding and addressing current concerns is a theme that can help us to gauge the nature of teachers' responses to recent reforms.

In exploring the nature of the 'personal past', several scholars have highlighted the close relationship between the individual and the social. The social framework of autobiographical memory has often appeared so important that individual or personal influences are virtually discounted as key factors in its development (Ross 1991). Tonkin suggests that the interconnections between memory, cognition and history help to shape individual selves and identities:

> Individuals are also social beings, formed in interaction, reproducing and also altering the societies of which they are members. I argue that 'the past' is not only a resource to deploy, to support a case or assert a social claim, it also enters memory in different ways and helps to structure it. Literate or illiterate, we are our memories. We also try to shape our futures in the light of past experience – or what we understand to have been past experience – and, representing how things were, we draw a social portrait, a model which is a reference list of what to follow and what to avoid.                                    (Tonkin 1992, p. 2)

She goes on to portray memory as being a part of a mediation between society and history, 'the site of the social practices that make us, together with the cognitive practices through which we understand society' (p. 12). This 'social structuration of recall', she insists, is basic both to the individual self and to social identity: 'Our intentions for the future are grounded in the past and without remembering we cannot see, for how else would we know what we see?' (p. 104).

Memory can be described as self-interested in the sense that individuals tend to employ it, whether knowingly or unconsciously, to help to justify not only their actions in the present, but also the general pattern of their lives. It is malleable in that it can and does alter in the light of changing events and circumstances. This is true both of individual memory and of the collective memory shared by society or a social group. As Tittler (1997) explains,

> The concept of collective memory derives from the notion that the members of particular social groups or generational cohorts inevitably share some collective notion of the past, and that this notion itself forms one of the defining elements of such groups or cohorts. But these shared memories are neither randomly formed nor immutable. The collective act of remembering remains a dynamic and highly subjective process, in which deliberate reconstruction is even more important than random recollection. What each group or

generation remembers depends very considerably on the requirements of its own time and place, especially as conceived by its leaders.                              (Tittler 1997, pp. 283–4)

The dynamic and subjective characteristics of collective memory have been the subject of much recent historical scrutiny. For example, according to Gay, 'Memory, we know, is the supple minister of self-interest, and collective memory is in this respect, as in others, like the memory of individuals' (Gay 1975, p. 206). Gay also notes that public history often constitutes a key device for the maintenance or, in other cases, the reorientation of the collective memory. Indeed, he suggests, 'Most collective memory is a convenient distortion or an equally convenient amnesia; it has all too often been the historian's assignment to assist his culture in remembering events that did not happen, and in forgetting events that did. The culture wants a past it can use' (p. 206). On the other hand, Nora seeks to draw a sharp distinction between memory as 'a phenomenon of the present', and history as 'a representation of the past' (Nora 1992, p. 3).

Historians have recently documented the importance of public artefacts such as war memorials in shaping and informing collective memories (e.g. Schama 1996; Wilson 1996; Young 1993), in a fashion that serves to justify the role of particular societies and to cultivate their sense of identity and solidarity as against other societies, nations or cultures. Other recent historical research has investigated the repression of collective memories with respect for example to the Holocaust, concentration camps and collaboration in the Second World War (e.g. Walston 1997). There are important parallels here with other recent research on individual memory that investigates its 'self-serving' and 'creative' features (e.g. Neisser and Fivush 1994), and that seeks to understand the nature of the so-called 'false memory syndrome' with respect to memories of child abuse (Prendergast 1997).

So far as teachers are concerned, the major work of Miriam Ben-Peretz has tellingly demonstrated the importance of memory in pursuing an understanding of teachers' knowledge. Her research with retired teachers in Israel has attempted to reconstruct what she calls 'the history of practice over time' (Ben-Peretz 1995, p. 3). Through a study of their memory of past events, she seeks to recover 'the basis for the construction and organisation of teachers' personal professional knowledge in a way that will allow them to use this knowledge' (pp. 7–8). The 'professional memories', that is to say, are the key to unlocking the 'wisdom of practice'. Ben-Peretz includes different forms of memory within this study, in particular 'episodic memory', equivalent to autobiographical memory, that relates to particular events, episodes or experiences, and 'semantic memory' that conveys a general knowledge about the world. She also evokes the notion of a 'script' that constitutes a set of guidelines for understanding life events. Such scripts, according to Ben-Peretz, 'provide a framework for remembering events and for acting upon these memories' (p. 11).

Ben-Peretz's account of teachers' memories tends to emphasize personalized, individual memory, and does not develop a strong connection between the personal and the social. It also seems to minimize the possible role of self-interest or broadly political explanations for the nature of memory (e.g. pp. 12–13). Both of these facets of recent historical scholarship and memory research need to be taken further in developing a fuller understanding of teachers' memories. It would be helpful also to strengthen the links that are suggested but not fully developed in Ben-Peretz's work between 'memory' and 'history', that is, to investigate the extent to which the historical memory of teachers helps to shape their ideas about teaching and about themselves as teachers. In doing so, there needs to be some conception of the relationship between the 'myths' that have surrounded the nature of teachers and teaching, and the memories that teachers have constructed to inform their practice and to sustain their identity. The myth of the 'secret garden of the curriculum' offers an interesting example of this relationship.


## THE GOOD OLD DAYS?

Teachers' control in the curriculum domain, as we have already seen, constitutes a central facet of the myth of teacher professionalism in England and Wales, symbolized in the rich imagery of the 'secret garden'. At the same time, it is associated with a particular historical period, well within the living memory of many teachers and other educators and policy-makers who have been adapting to the changed circumstances of the 1990s. It appears therefore to be a promising instance of an area in which myth and memory coalesce, and it may be instructive to discover how teachers understand and interpret its significance.

As part of a wider study of teachers' professional cultures funded by the ESRC, secondary school teachers were asked in a semi-structured interview situation to explain the changes in their freedom and autonomy in the curriculum domain that have come about as a result of the policy changes of the past decade (see Appendix). Responses to a specific prompt on whether there had ever been a 'golden age' of teaching revealed an active recall of the earlier period. These both incorporated the myth of teacher professionalism, and sought to make sense of current developments in a way that would allow teachers, individually and collectively, to develop a clear role in the future. In some cases, these responses were nostalgic and supportive of the myth, tending to evoke a lost 'golden age'. In others, however, some hostility was expressed about the role of teachers and the nature of teaching before the introduction of the National Curriculum, implying the existence of what might be called a 'state of nature' that the National Curriculum had come into existence to order and tame.

In these interviews, the idea of teacher freedom in the curriculum, where it is recognized at all, is closely associated with the role of teachers before the introduction of the National Curriculum. Where they are new to teaching and so have no direct experience of teaching before the National Curriculum, they often rely on media reports or on the stories of colleagues, and on memories of their own schooldays. One secondary school history teacher in his second year of teaching, for example, notes: 'I'm only getting it second hand but they did seem to teach what they wanted to teach, and they could choose their schemes of work, that sounds quite appealing, you know.' He bases this view on information from a close teaching colleague at the same school about 'life before the National Curriculum'. The idea of being able to 'choose yourself' what to teach is attractive to this teacher: 'I mean there are parts of the National Curriculum which I wouldn't want to teach.' As a beginning teacher the previous year, 'there was the odd occasion when I thought, "Oh, I'm not teaching that today, I'll skip that lot, I'll come back to it", but apart from that you know, you teach what you are told'.

Other teachers also experienced a sense of regret at the apparent loss of 'professional' freedom. One geography teacher, a head of department, recalls that before the National Curriculum, 'I think there was a lot more freedom, I mean, all schools had different, lower school curriculums, there was so much freedom but I mean within a school you would have to all stick to the same thing, otherwise it would have made exams and use of resources, purchasing of resources, so difficult.' In this instance, external accountability especially as represented by Ofsted inspections in the climate of the 1990s appears to be oppressive in nature, as the teacher continues:

> I think that perhaps now, there always seems to be somebody, somewhere over my shoulder, looking over my shoulder. It's a long time now but thinking back prior to the National Curriculum, you did your own thing and you did your own thing with the best intentions, you wanted the pupils to move forward academically, geographical knowledge and so on, but now you've got a ladder to climb and it's almost like gladiators climbing the wall and you feel there's somebody behind you and if you don't make the right steps they'll be on you.

He is specific about who the 'gladiators' are:

> It's not the school. It's not the head teacher .... It's not the school now it's, I suppose the Ofsted inspector is the one that you're wondering all the time, are you up to the standard that they are setting. Not really sure of what that standard is. So that's the concern, that's the worry.

For this teacher, the 'freedom' that had been enjoyed before the introduction of the National Curriculum has diminished so far as to make the idea of 'teacher freedom in the curriculum' meaningless in the changed context of the 1990s, as the following exchange reflects:

> Q. In the 1990s, what does the idea of teacher freedom in the curriculum mean to you?
> A. Say it again, teacher ... ?
> Q. What does the idea of teacher freedom in the curriculum mean to you?
> A. Nothing. Is it a term that's bandied about? Or have you just made ... it is one that you've made up?

In this case, then, while the memory of teacher freedom is still strong, and although the teacher has a notion of a lost 'golden age' before the National Curriculum, the experience of rapid change is such as to render the application of the ideal literally meaningless in the context of the 1990s.

Some other teachers also look back to a 'golden age' of teacher control in the curriculum domain. One, a female technology teacher and head of department, reflects on when she was herself a pupil at a grammar school: 'I simply chose what subjects I wanted to do.' By contrast, 'Now that would be frowned on now because they would say that you wouldn't get your broad balance of curriculum and you would tend to specialize too early. They've sort of gone against that now.' In this way, she suggests, 'there's no freedom and I think that as teachers, most teachers are far happier with the idea that they can make decisions about what is taught and they don't abuse that'. Indeed, she insists,

> they resent a lot the fact that somebody else is telling them, not subject content but the framework and things and they would deal just as happily and would take it just as responsibly without any government interference at all because I think on the whole they do take their job seriously, they are responsible people and they would value greater freedom. They would value the trust. I think it's this resentment of not being trusted that really does the damage.

Another female technology teacher similarly looks back to what she calls the 'good old days', 'when if the sun shone you could go outside and do something you wanted to do, rather than something that you had to do in the classroom'. She suggests that 'I suppose really, I was being selfish because I like being outside but I don't think the kids suffered, I mean they were always working and always learning.' It was 'just more fun sometimes to do what you wanted to do on the spur of the moment rather than think, well we've got to do this today'. Since the introduction of the National Curriculum 'there's not the freedom to experiment and see how things would go'. Thus for example, whereas previously she could swap over her two subject areas of art and technology and combine them, this was now more difficult: 'You can't just do a joint project because you feel like it and you couldn't do it with just one group of students to see how it went because they would then be lacking in some knowledge that they'd need for the next stage.' Similar views are expressed by a male technology teacher:

> Before there was a national curriculum and when I first started teaching in '75 you could go into the classroom, close the door and you were the be all and end all within that classroom. Now that was, that is nowadays totally unacceptable because there is no control if you like but it was based on a principle of trust, professional trust, a sense of professionalism which is what we're talking about.

This notion of 'professional trust' is also raised by a male mathematics teacher who harks back to a 'golden age in teaching' in the 1970s, when 'I think that we were valued as professionals more'. At that time, according to this teacher, 'We felt that we were being paid as professionals and I think there was a little bit more breathing space to do things extremely well.' For example, 'sometimes I think you may in the past have had a chance to talk about the child x or y if he or she has a particular problem', but he finds that there is now less communication about such matters, so that 'sometimes we can't give quite the support that we may have been able to do in the past'. Compared to when he started teaching, in 1968, 'I think we're regarded less as professionals now. I think that under the present [Conservative] government certainly, teachers have been seen as whipping boys and girls, in that a lot of society's failings are put on the shoulders of teachers rather than on the family.'

In the testimony of these teachers, the memory of the 'good old days' comes across strongly as a time of professional trust and relative freedom to experiment. Teacher professionalism is linked explicitly to these ideals. In contrast, the restrictions of the National Curriculum and the need to be accountable to the 'gladiators' of Ofsted mean an undermining of this version of professionalism. The professional memory of these teachers, including some who have little or no direct experience of teaching before the National Curriculum, indicates a residual but still active influence on their approach to teaching and their identity as teachers.

## DOMINOES AND KNITTING

On the other hand, for some others the supposed curtailment of this freedom comes across as no great loss, or more positively as a means of providing greater account-ability, suggesting a different operating version of professionalism. According to one male geography teacher, for example,

> Teacher freedom? It's quite interesting. I think it's been cut back, I think the National Curriculum has had an effect on that. I don't think that's a bad thing either . . . . I felt as though well, I'm teaching it this way and sort of the results are coming through this way and

another, nobody's questioning me. How are you doing that? You know, this was in the old, but the National Curriculum I feel as though it's knocked the ideas around as I would suggest and pulled us more into line so that hopefully most of us are doing the same thing or similarly the same thing.

This teacher also suggests that external inspections give him the opportunity to discuss, defend and improve his teaching: 'At the same time I'd argue with anybody that was to come into the classroom and maybe I'll be arguing next October when we get inspected, that if he or she says, "well why do you, why are you off course here?", I'll explain why.'

In another case, a recently appointed female history teacher, trained under the National Curriculum, is also highly critical of the previous regime, a view based as she admits on 'my perception of when I was at school':

It was much more chalk and talk, it was much more like, well, let's write something on the blackboard and disappear to the staffroom for a cup of tea and that's gone. Well it should have gone. There's still some members of staff who do that but I think especially in history at least you have to do more, in fact, varied in the way that you teach it ... the introduction of the National Curriculum has made people really have to sit up and think about what they are teaching and I think that makes you think about how you're going to teach it.

This means, she continues, that 'you could have had a department going on for twenty years teaching exactly the same thing in exactly the same way but all of a sudden along comes a new programme of study that you've got to teach so I think it's made people sit up and think, well am I doing this as well as I could, could I do it in a better way?' In this instance, however, there is also a strong sense of loss as the teacher evokes as one aspect of teachers' lives before the National Curriculum 'sitting in the staff room, blooming playing dominoes and knitting', and contrasts this with the present situation: 'if I went into the staff room and started knitting that would be it, my name would be mud in this school. "Where has she got the time from to do that knitting?"' Then she reflects:

Shame really because ... the school spirit isn't there as much because you haven't got time to socialize. I mean you haven't got time to really get to know other people. It's taken me two and a half years to make real friends in this school .... Yes so I think that's hard as well especially if you're new to the profession and things. It's hard to adjust to. Because you don't see people. I mean you're there five minutes having your cup of tea at break after you've finished sorting out all the kids who haven't done their homework and then the next minute you're back in the classroom and everyone's off in their own direction you know? We only have a 35-minute dinner break and it's a split dinner so you might not see anyone one day and you're back teaching again.

Another female teacher, in mathematics, remembers her early years of teaching and again compares these unfavourably with the present:

When I started teaching, I can remember being given a maths handbook which had obviously been in circulation for several years and we just worked through it every year and I should think that we did that for about four years while I was at that school and it had obviously been used in previous years so every year the first year got taught exactly the same thing and every year the second year got taught the same thing and we used the same textbooks.

By contrast,

nowadays we rewrite our schemes of work every year and we're expected to have policies on this, that and the other so we actually discuss these sorts of things at much greater length. We look more at how we teach them than when I started teaching. When I started teaching we were given a textbook which we worked through from cover to cover and then we went through the next textbook and worked through that from cover to cover and we taught it as the textbook did it. I think we have meetings now where we discuss 'well, how did you do this, and how do you do that?' and we use a variety of textbooks, the children don't have their own. So yes, it's changed a lot.

This change she therefore sees as 'beneficial', especially because as she says, 'I think that it was fairly boring when I started, "We'll all turn to page 6 and we'll all do this."' Moreover, she adds, there was also a certain laxity in attitudes when she started teaching: 'I can also remember, I mean when I started the summer term used to be regarded as a nice soft option. That has totally gone now, totally. I mean I used to mark 'O' level papers in the summer. I wouldn't even contemplate it now. I mean there just would not be the time.' This was a clear improvement, in her view, as she answers whether there was ever a golden age for teachers: 'It's now.'

There is a strong tendency in all of these examples to idealize the role of teachers in the curriculum domain before the National Curriculum, that is, to caricature it either as idyllic in its scope for freedom and autonomy to 'do your own thing', or as something naive, irresponsible and dangerous, all 'dominoes and knitting'. Whether nostalgic or hostile, however, these perceptions add powerfully to the impression that the National Curriculum has transformed the position of teachers for good or ill. They thereby reinforce two professional myths: that in the past curriculum freedom was virtually unlimited, and that now they have little or no scope to assert their own authority. The myth of teacher professionalism has fused with the memory of change to create a resilient impression that acts as a basis or framework for teachers to respond to their everyday challenges.

## THE POLITICS OF PEDAGOGY

It is also important to note that although there is a widespread notion of change, many of these teachers still experienced a considerable degree of continuity in their own teaching. In the case of the geography teacher who regretted the loss of autonomy involved in the National Curriculum, the view is expressed that the National Curriculum has actually made very little difference to his own teaching: 'My views of what makes a good lesson have matured ... so the way I teach will certainly have changed over twenty years but only through my own development. I can't say that National Curriculum has actually altered the way I teach.' Moreover, he also indicates several areas of scope for manoeuvre so far as the content of the geography curriculum is concerned. The 'constraints' are clear, he suggests,

> In that there are certain topics that have to be done like, for instance, earthquakes. I know I've got to do earthquakes. If I had a complete hatred of doing earthquakes it wouldn't matter, I'd still have to do it. So there are those sort of topics that have got to be covered. There's freedom in things like, a developing country has got to be studied and you've got flexibility to choose the developing country. But a developing country must be done, so there's the constraint, although there's freedom within that.

On the other hand, in this case at least the National Curriculum did not entail a major change in content:

> Certain bits were the same. I've actually saved all the schemes of work, lower school syllabuses that I've had like for the past twenty years and I can easily look back. But for instance, just before coming down here I was teaching a piece of work about manufacturing industry and I know, I can picture it on a previous syllabus I did, exactly the same thing. Exactly the same thing.

Overall, although the National Curriculum had 'widened the type of topics I've done and widened the scale', this geography teacher describes himself as 'happy with what the National Curriculum asks me to teach' (see also Roberts 1995; 1997, on geography teachers and the National Curriculum).

There is a significant disparity here between the lessons gleaned from myth and memory, which give the impression of rapid change and qualitative loss or improvement, and the everyday experience of teaching, which suggests continuity and gradual development. In another case, that of a recently appointed male history teacher, there is a similar sense of a major change from the situation that prevailed before the National Curriculum, but again some indications of scope for manoeuvre in spite of the prescribed limitations of the curriculum framework. This teacher points out that 'in a lot of it you haven't a lot of choice of what goes in, it's prescribed in the National Curriculum', although he had himself 're-jigged and re-vamped' some of the schemes of work at his school 'to try to make them more interesting'. On the other hand, he also notes that 'within limited areas, within assessment and within content we can make some decisions'. In particular, he continues, 'there are times when the National Curriculum is not that precisely worded, it's vague'. If there is a list of options for study on a particular topic, for example, 'you don't necessarily need to cover them all, so we are making decisions in that sort of area, "oh we won't do that, it's not as good as this"', say'. This scope for negotiation was especially important in relation to teaching methods, as he continues:

> You still have to teach, you still have to teach the lessons every day, it's still your job, that you were trained for and despite the fact that they're telling you what you've got to do, they can't make you do it in a certain way. You still make the ultimate decision that I'm going to present this through a work sheet or I'm going to talk about it or I'm going to dress up as a whatever, or I'm going to show them a video about it or whatever. Or I'm going to do it through drama, you know, you still make the decision at, you know sort of the front line level but this is how I'm going to do it. They've told me I've got to teach to the Reformation but they haven't said that I can't dress up as, I mean I haven't, but they can't tell me how I've got to do it as it were. You know, if I want to pretend that I'm Martin Luther, then I will . . . .

Again there seems to be a strong tension at work here between the myth and memory of teacher professionalism, and the everyday experience of teaching.

The Dearing Review of the National Curriculum, which proposed reducing the amount of prescribed material in the National Curriculum in order to 'give more scope for professional judgement' (Dearing 1993, p. 17), also influenced the views of secondary school teachers in several instances, often stirring comparisons with teaching before the introduction of the National Curriculum. One geography teacher, generally favourable to the effects of the National Curriculum, reflects that following the Dearing Review,

> I'm more comfortable in the sense that . . . there seems to be less content . . . . And there seems to be a greater chance of us, shall I say for instance, of using our own materials again. Sort of we're in if you like, more control. Particularly say for instance in the initial stages in years seven and eight.

In the case of an experienced male mathematics teacher, the Dearing Review is an encouragement to 'professionalism' in so far as it is not 'prescriptive' and because 'it gives you a direction rather than a straitjacket'.

This is again the case with another experienced male mathematics teacher, a head of department who has witnessed the changing scene of the past thirty years. He is critical of the scope for freedom that he recalls before the introduction of the National Curriculum: 'I fully accept that in the English education system perhaps there's been far too much scope. People have been able to do what they want, operate whichever syllabuses they wanted and there's not been the core requirements.' The same teacher is concerned that the balance has gone too far the other way in favour of accountability and external control, but he is encouraged by the Dearing Review to think that 'perhaps we recognize that we've had too much freedom, but I don't think we want to give up the professional judgemental situation that we find ourselves in'. This teacher also notes a high degree of continuity in his own teaching over the years. To this teacher, mathematics is unique in that its content is 'a body of knowledge that is relatively unchanging, certainly as far as a secondary school curriculum is concerned'. For this reason, 'Parents may not recognize the way maths is taught today, but essentially mathematics is the same .... I don't teach it the way I did twenty years ago but what I teach hasn't changed very much.' With this experience and with the control of an 'unchanging' body of knowledge now encouraged further by the Dearing Review, this teacher has the confidence to assert that 'I'm an experienced teacher, perhaps too old to change too much, I don't know, and I find that I can carry on perhaps more in the way that I did, and maybe some people expect me to get away with it.'


MEMORY AND POLICY

It is useful to compare these teachers' memories with those of a range of key policy-makers and opinion-formers who were interviewed as part of the same research study (see Appendix). These key informants also expressed different kinds of memory about the position of teachers before the Education Reform Act of 1988, and these also helped to form the basis for their ideas about current problems relating to teachers. Essentially, these fell into three distinct groups: those who felt the pre-1988 regime was a golden age of professionalism that needed to be regained, those who felt that teacher freedom before 1988 had gone too far but that restrictions since 1988 had also been too strong, and those who were strongly critical of the previous situation and felt that the position had improved since 1988.

The first group, consisting of those who regretted a loss of teacher freedom especially in the curriculum domain, included for example a chief education officer and former secondary school teacher whose wife is a deputy headteacher in a primary school. He argued that the reforms of the 1990s have reduced the role of teachers from that of a 'professional' to that of a 'technician', especially because of what he considers 'a serious interference in the content of the profession'. In part, he suggests, this is due to a widespread image of teachers which is that 'they're all kind of softly liberal and still in the nineteen-sixties, you know, go home and put their flares on and smoke pot every night or something and it really isn't like that in schools'. The problem with the Schools Council curriculum projects of the 1960s, according to this official, was that teachers were not sufficiently involved in them. An attempt to 'make any difference to class-room practice' would require such involvement rather than a 'confrontational basis'. Only active involvement in such reforms would allow teachers to, as he puts it, 'reclaim professionalism back'.

This preference for the past was also shared by a former senior Labour politician and teacher who stressed the 'courage' and spontaneity of individual teachers. He contends that James Callaghan's Ruskin speech of 1976 and the 'Great Debate' that followed had 'killed off' the earlier 'fifties and sixties and early seventies professionalism, which I liked'. Since that time, and especially in the past decade, 'teachers' courage has changed, teachers' courage has been weakened', so that 'teachers aren't making decisions, their own decisions, about the curriculum, which they ought to be'. This means the teacher being able to say,

> I'm going to jump the rest of the lesson and talk about one thing that really interests these kids and then five minutes before the lessons ends, say, right, you've wasted twenty minutes of my time, diverting me onto this, this is your homework tonight, you will do this, that and the other and if anyone simply doesn't understand this problem, come and see me now.

Such a 'split second decision' would not be allowed now because of the 'fear of inspection': 'And that's gone ... you're in line management to some extent now in the sense that you weren't in the past.' Indeed, he argues, 'that's what I always felt was the great empowering thing, you walked into that classroom, you shut that door and you were the king and there was nobody going to inspect you, like nobody'.

The second set of memories among these key informants revolved around the view that the notion of the teacher as the 'king' who could not be inspected had been too extreme and damaging before 1988, but that the reaction against this approach since 1988 had tended to be too severe. This was the stance for example of a prominent teachers' union leader. To this official, teacher freedom had previously been excessive and this had led to difficulties: 'there is some evidence that allowing teachers to do their own thing was leading to perhaps too much diversity'. For example,

> I know of cases where like in a primary school for three successive years there was a lot of overlap, they taught the Norman Conquest for three successive years ... now quite clearly teachers were being left to get on with their own thing and, that's fine to a point but there should have been someone looking at everyone's work and saying, well ... this class was taught the Norman Conquest last year, doesn't make sense to be taught the Norman Conquest again this year.

However, in seeking to coordinate the management of the curriculum the government had moved in and 'creates as many problems as they were trying to solve in so doing'. According to this union official, it was right for the government and for parliament to be able to ensure that schools and teachers were accountable, but

> then after that discretion should be left to schools to determine what subjects are going to be taught and you know, to what degree ... it's a shame we couldn't have worked out a decent system between ourselves but because of the lack of trust and then the government moved in and prescribed all kinds of things and this is what is I think rightly perceived as an expression of lack of confidence in teachers' professionalism.

In this process, teacher autonomy, which may never have existed as the myths suggest, 'has certainly been destroyed'.

Similarly, a former senior HMI argued that before 1988 too many anomalies had been evident and this had justified new 'curriculum law': 'there was no doubt that our curriculum was stupidly varied and those big HMI reports of '89 on secondary and primary education maths revealed that there was so much variation in what an individual youngster might meet, or the resources they'd get or whatever, that it was just indefensible'. It had been important to establish a 'new balance', not so much because everyone was critical of what the schools were doing, but because they 'simply didn't know what they were doing'. However, in redressing this problem, the 'trust' and 'discretion' that had been formerly accorded to teachers had also been lost, and this needed to be regained: 'I think we're going to have to trust teachers eventually … I mean those curriculum and assessment issues will have to be addressed.'

A senior Conservative member of parliament with strong educational connections expressed largely similar sentiments. He has another view of what was going wrong before 1988, which is that there was too much egalitarian theory influencing the schools. He remembers talking to a professor of education 'who was doing a piece of research and the basis of his theory was that there should be no testing before degree level'. It had been necessary to insist on rigorous testing and assessment in order to counter such influences. On the other hand, teachers needed to retain some sense of 'ownership', and the curriculum should not become 'completely rigid'. Moreover, a renewal of trust was needed in order for teachers to do their job:

> We can tell a teacher *what* to teach but they can't tell a teacher *how* to teach, because once a teacher goes into his or her classroom, that's it. Even the head or anybody else, nobody can stand with them twenty four hours a day, so you rely upon the teachers themselves and their teaching style and methodology etc., but the parents to feel that they can come along and start to question the nuts and bolts of the profession, I think, has not been the most helpful way.

In general, to this politician, 'trying to get the balance right between that professional judgement which a good teacher will exercise in his or her classroom, or his or her school if he/she is a headteacher, and the prescription which is there in the National Curriculum, is the trick'.

For a third group of key informants, however, such memories and the lessons that they instilled were thoroughly misguided. To these, not only had the situation before 1988 been unacceptable, but reform had been largely on the right lines and the position of teachers had improved as a result. This was the view, for example, of a former senior official of the National Curriculum Council. This informant had in fact some personal prior insight as his father was a headmaster and 'believed nobody should go into a teacher's classroom because they were the king there and that everything they said went'. His father had believed 'that professionalism therefore implied was the curriculum was entirely at the discretion of the teacher and that judgement about classroom practice was entirely for the individual professional'. Such a view, according to this respondent, was 'one idea in the extreme'. However, it had led to major problems, especially as 'the vast majority of teachers didn't think very much about what they were doing'. In particular, he insists,

> the more you talked to teachers at INSET training courses, the more you were convinced they never thought fundamentally about what the curriculum was for, what was it, what was in it for them? What was in it for children? What was in it for the community? What was in it for the economic state of the nation? None of these things I think ever crossed

their minds and therefore the paradox is that, out of total freedom came a kind of voluntary or involuntary imprisonment through lack of thought.

The onset of the National Curriculum had changed this situation for the better: 'ironically having to think about the curriculum, it's quite a sophisticated fact, has forced teachers to be more professional and I think it's forced the best of them to realize how far they can exploit these freedoms'. Therefore 'basically within a defined envelope and that's a big, limiting factor but within a very large defined envelope', teachers would have more freedom, discrimination and choice as a result of the reforms.

Another senior official at the School Curriculum and Assessment Authority pursues a broadly similar argument about teachers in the 1970s and 1980s largely lacking reflective skills:

> I think in the past, in the really good old days that some people fantasize about, that teachers were often not at all reflective .... . I mean people in the past were jolly, jolly unreflective often about what they were doing and one of the very good things I think about the last twenty or thirty years is that people have had to think much more about what they are doing and justify what they are doing rather more than they did. And that has been a good thing and I think generally schools are much more effective institutions, and ask far more questions and query their own practice far more than they did.

Teachers were becoming more 'professional' as a result of this development, rather than reverting to become 'mechanics': 'the context has changed with the coming of the National Curriculum but to suggest that somehow we've reduced teachers to mere mechanics ... who just sort of go in and do the page of the National Curriculum on a particular day that they are required to do it is absolute nonsense'.

A senior official at the Teacher Training Agency echoes this perception of an improvement and continuing development of teachers' professionalism over the past twenty years. Before the National Curriculum, she argues, most teachers made little use of their apparent freedom: 'The average teachers and less good teachers simply took up the textbook and worked from the beginning of the textbook to the end.' Moreover, there was a 'proliferation of courses', with too many undemanding syllabuses that 'did no service to the children who went through those'. Indeed, she continues,

> I, for one, spent much of my time getting rid of three thousand of those syllabuses and I certainly don't want to bring them back. I do not believe that the teachers should be able to say 'I will be the teacher, I will decide the curriculum, I will decide the pedagogy, I will decide the assessment, I will decide the qualifications.' I think that's totally unacceptable.

The 1988 Education Reform Act had 'replaced those sort of curricula with the National Curriculum and very many teachers have welcomed it'. In general, according to this official, 'The coming of the 1988 Education Act provided a curriculum structure that was better than one could get out of textbooks, and for the good teachers it freed them up to develop their pedagogy in relation to a curriculum framework which was given them.' Therefore the 1988 Act was not about 'deskilling teachers', but, on the contrary, 'I see it as providing a blueprint against which they can develop what is their true professionalism.' On this perspective, the 'true professionalism' of the future stands in stark contrast to the false prospectuses of the past.

CONCLUSIONS

The example of secondary school teachers in the curriculum domain in the English context highlights the close relationship of 'myth' and 'memory', which reinforce each other in a symbiotic manner. The overall effect is a powerful impression of change that helps to inform teachers' assessment of their situation in the 1990s. More than this, myth and memory combine in the construction of teachers' identity, both individual and social.

The images produced by myth and memory are highly idealized. A favourable version of the past conjures up a golden age, while a hostile image gives a negative stereotype of teachers before the introduction of the National Curriculum. In neither version is there a strong sense of complexity or contestation in the position of teachers in the curriculum domain in the 1950s, 1960s and 1970s. Such ambiguities and complexities are edited out of the picture, are forgotten. In the same process, underlying continuities are obscured by the vividness of the contrasts. The myths are too pervasive to allow for such complications, while the memories are influenced both by the framework of the myths and by the social and political context of the 'remembering self'. In such a circumstance, it is not surprising that there may be major contradictions not only between the myth and the reality of 'what really happened', but also between the memories and the documentary records. This in turn suggests important tensions between myth, memory and history that need to be addressed in detail in further research on teachers' thinking and professional identities.

The range of memories articulated by the policy-makers, politicians and influential observers relate in an interesting way to those of the secondary school teachers interviewed for this study. They are looking back on older forms of teacher professionalism associated with the 'secret garden', and are using their memories and experiences both to make sense of ambiguities and contradictions, and to suggest current needs and opportunities. In so doing they highlight three broad currents of opinion on the received version of teacher professionalism, which one key informant described as the 'earlier fifties and sixties and early seventies professionalism'. The first approach was that of the diehard or conservative, resolute in their determination to retain or revise what they saw as the ideals and practices of the past, and to resist those of the present. The second was that of the reformer or reconstructionist, who wished to select the most important elements of this received tradition and adapt them to a changing context and new demands. Third were the radicals who dismissed the past and sought to erect a new set of ideals and practices in place of the old. It is here that the older professionalism characteristic of the 1950s and 1960s came into clear opposition with aspirations for a 'new professionalism' that have arisen in the 1990s. We will observe some of the ideas involved in this latter movement emerging in greater detail in Part 2 of this study.

*Part 2*

---

# The New Era

# Introduction

In Part 1 it was shown how curriculum autonomy has been a major focus of the study of the public politics of teacher professionalism over the past 50 years – curriculum autonomy has been used as a sensitive indicator of the way the currents of teacher autonomy and teacher professionalism have flowed. Other indicators could have been chosen, although it might be said that they would have been less sensitive, less important and less well documented. Alongside this examination of control of the curriculum, change and continuities have been explored, and myths of professionalism have been counterpoised with some of the realities, principally through study of documentary sources.

Part 2 explores these themes in a more finely textured way, concentrating on the ways in which they have been manifested in the past fifteen years. It is largely based on oral evidence about secondary school teaching in England. Although continuing to recognize the importance of the school curriculum in shaping teachers' work, the second part of the book makes more of the larger raft of educational changes which have shaped the setting in which there continues to be contestation of teacher professionalism. It is accompanied by fears of deprofessionalization which are juxtaposed with claims that the turn of the millennium will see, at least in Britain, the emergence of a 'new professionalism'. Whilst Chapter 5 continues to focus essentially on a broad interpretation of 'curriculum', the issue of curriculum content is shown to be of decreasing significance in terms of teachers' sense of professionalism, whilst concerns over curriculum method or pedagogy are gaining ground. The argument is that, whilst teachers' autonomy may have been circumscribed by policy changes over curriculum content, other important aspects of the curriculum remain outside of policy control. The 'delivered' curriculum is seen to be less amenable to regulation than is the planned curriculum. Furthermore, schools, departments and even individual teachers have all interpreted policies in different ways and those ways have changed over time. It is unwise to make sweeping statements about policy changes and teacher autonomy.

Chapter 6 starts with the premise that no amount of professional development, not even the grand developmental sequence envisaged by the 'new professionalism' Green Paper in Britain, can ensure fidelity of implementation (Fullan 1991). Changes themselves get changed in the process of transmission through a system, partly because there are variations in the meanings of the innovation that implementers construct and partly because plans have to be adapted to a range of different settings. Just as departmental management is constrained by contingencies (Turner and Bolam 1998), so the possibilities for change are similarly bounded. That said, if there is a lack of opportunities for teachers to learn about the change and to develop well-conceived ways of trying to make it work, then what happens in the classroom will be even further removed from what planners intended. The argument is that one reason why the implementation of National Curriculum policies has been so fraught is because in-service provision has been inadequate. The case developed in this chapter also has important implications for attempts to implement the National Curriculum for the millennium and for attempts to improve education generally.

In Chapter 7, we draw together a number of themes as we explore the extent to which teaching can still be seen as a profession. This is considered from the points of view of secondary teachers of different subjects, and of thirteen key informants, people close to recent curriculum policy-making. Although there is evidence of a diversity of views, it is safe to say that the question of whether reductions in teacher control mean that teaching is less of a profession is a dead question. There is near-consensus that changes in curriculum-making powers have not deprofessionalized teaching, partly because the realities of this power were, as Chapter 3 showed, different from the myths. Yet it would be a mistake to reach closure on the basis of this one sensitive indicator alone, since a striking feature of the past fifteen years has been the busyness of government, reaching deep into the workings of schools. This complex of actions is reviewed, leading to the conclusion that teaching may have been deprofessionalized, and that if it hasn't, then teacher professionalism is certainly a different thing than it was fifteen years ago. The raft of changes that has drifted across all areas of teachers' working lives includes:

- several versions of a National Curriculum with their associated assessment arrangements
- the marketization of education
- the growth of managerialism
- changes in terms and conditions of service (for example, appraisal, contractual specification of duties, continuing moves towards performance-related pay)
- the loss of disproportionate numbers of older, more experienced teachers and the growth in numbers of part-time teachers and those on fixed-term contracts
- an inspection system that is widely seen as punitive
- changes to in-service education provision
- increased control of initial teacher education
- repeated calls for people without professional qualifications to be allowed to take on some – or all – teaching functions

To that incomplete list we add that we heard from many teachers who believe that they are faced with increasing numbers of children who have special needs, whose behaviour is so bad that they have to be suspended or excluded from school, or who simply are not keen on schooling.

There are two remarks we wish to make about this list. Individually, each change might have a greater or lesser impact on any school, department or teacher. Taken together they have what systems theory calls 'emergent properties'. That means that they have a force that is far greater than could be appreciated by simply adding them together. So, we cannot, in this part of the book, treat curriculum in isolation, as much of the PCT data reminded us. So, many teachers did not see that the reduction in their control of curriculum content significantly reduced their autonomy, which they frequently associated with control of pedagogy. Yet, as Chapter 5 shows, although the National Curriculum did not constrain pedagogy (arguably in some subjects it encouraged 'progressive' pedagogies), other changes did reduce practical autonomy in this vital area.

One qualification is necessary. A host of structural changes certainly alters the objective work environment. However, it would be rash then to make generalizations about their impact on teachers since they can deliberately or unwittingly resist those changes. In any case, policies always change as they are translated into practice and this is all the more so in 'loose-coupled' systems, where there are high levels of uncertainty in daily practice and where practitioners therefore have to make a large number of non-routine decisions or judgements. This is compounded by the continual swirl of thinking at the level of policy: Kliebard (1987) has shown how the American curriculum has been contested by four groups and Lawton (1993) has done a similar task in respect of curriculum policy-making in Britain.

The final chapter, mindful of these points, contains a consideration of the prospects for teaching taking on a 'new professionalism'. The chances of success depend, of course, on the match between the meaning of 'new professionalism' and the conditions in which teachers work. Recent discussions of 'new professionalism' have shown that while there might be agreement that old arguments about how to describe teachers' work have become sterile, there is little agreement about what teaching could and should involve in times of inexorable and ubiquitous change. Existing conditions, ideologies, politics and practices are so varied that different trajectories can be predicted for teaching in England, Ontario, Texas, Japan and Sweden, for example.

An interesting and perhaps complementary approach to the politics of professionalism looks to the way teachers feel. We have no doubt that teaching requires the application of complex knowledge and skill in non-routine situations that require quick and complex judgements. In that sense, it is a profession, and a high degree of classroom autonomy is assumed. Yet, if teachers do not feel appreciated, trusted and fulfilled, then can teaching still be seen as a profession? Can teaching be seen as a profession if the psychic rewards that have attracted people to it dematerialize, and if teachers find that their motivation to do anything more than comply crumbles like a chalk cliff into the sea?

# Chapter 5

# Curriculum Control and Teacher Professionalism

Despite the barrage of recent reforms affecting all parts of the state education system, in England and elsewhere, the school curriculum remains a crucial site of contestation in the battle to define the nature of teacher professionalism. The first part of this book provided a broad-brush view of the way that teacher control of curriculum content became prominent in discourse about teaching's occupational standing. However, curriculum is about more than content, comprising what is taught, how it is taught, how it is organized and how it is assessed. In the past fifteen years in England teachers' claims to curriculum control – and hence to professional standing – have moved from claims to control the content of the curriculum (although some scope for choice still remains) to claims to control the organization and teaching of material mandated by the government. Furthermore, control of assessment arrangements has been disputed with teacher action in protest at these arrangements leading to the Dearing review of the National Curriculum as a whole. In short, the curriculum, understood in its broadest sense, is central in shaping what teachers do on a day-to-day basis. Indeed Connell (1985, p. 87) argues that the school curriculum actually constitutes 'a definition of teachers' work'. This chapter examines in some detail the ways that teachers have experienced changes in their control of the curriculum and shows how the prevalent discourses and myths about professionalism have changed in the past fifteen years. From that base, it will later be suggested that change continues and that new discourses are becoming widespread and that new myths may be coalescing.

## CURRICULUM CONTROL AND DEPROFESSIONALIZATION

Given the centrality of curriculum to teachers' work and, particularly in the English context, to perceptions of teacher professionalism, then the sudden and enforced imposition of a prescribed National Curriculum for all state schools through the 1988 Education Reform Act might be viewed as a *de facto* deprofessionalization of the teaching force. However, such a view involves a gross oversimplification of reality and ignores important aspects of the complex and contested relationship between teachers and the state.

First, it assumes that 'professionalism' is a clear-cut concept that can be related in a straightforward way to certain attributes and, especially in this case, to the exercise of autonomy. Under this formulation, teachers who are granted autonomy in their work are judged to be 'professional', whilst those who are expected to follow instructions are not. Whilst this is in line with a traditional functionalist view of professionalism, which tended to define it largely in terms of the perceived characteristics of existing professions, and most notably those of the more established professions such as law and medicine in the USA and UK, more recent work on the subject has been much more critical of this ideal-type approach (see, for example, Torstendahl and Burrage 1990; Burrage and Torstendahl 1990). Comparative study underlines the social, cultural and historical diversity amongst different professions in different contexts and suggests that the notion of professionalism, far from being an absolute, is a social construct that, because of its connotations of power and privilege, is subject to constant contestation. On the one hand, for example, governments may employ the ideology of professionalism as a means of 'indirect rule' over the teaching force (Lawn and Ozga 1986), whilst on the other, occupational groups may use it as part of a strategy to enhance their position in the labour market.

Second, the idea of occupational autonomy is problematic, particularly in the public services whose employees are licensed to practice by the state. As Murphy (1990) points out, direct management is not the only form of control, and professionals may be socialized into desired behaviours by their training and by individual incentives which allow them to exercise only *relative* autonomy, a process which is further threatened by increased state regulation, which is evident in all western countries and across all professions. As we have observed, irrespective of the myths, the notion of relative autonomy is appropriate. Even during the supposed 'golden age' of teacher professionalism in England in the 1950s and 1960s, teachers' freedom was constrained by a number of factors, including the organizational demands of the school, over whose goals and administration they had only limited influence (Hoyle 1974). And to echo Chapter 3, their supposed control of the curriculum was limited by the requirements of university-based examinations boards and by the highly normative traditions of established academic subjects, as well as by the reluctance of many teachers actively to exploit their potential autonomy in this domain. Conversely, the supposed period of 'deprofessionalization' in the wake of the 1988 Education Reform Act was marked by an ultimate reliance upon teachers to translate these reforms into practice in real schools and real classrooms. The inevitable complexity of these situations, and the consequent need for non-routine decision-making, helped to create 'spaces for manoeuvre' (Bowe *et al.* 1992) within which teachers could continue to exercise their professional judgements. Thus teacher autonomy is not, in practice, an absolute whose presence or absence can be used to determine teacher professionalism: instead, there are varying degrees of autonomy which relate to different aspects of teachers' work and which may change over time and be different from school to school and from teacher to teacher.

A third point, closely related to that, is that claims that teachers are becoming automatically deprofessionalized as a result of government attempts to reassert control over the school curriculum ignore their active role in responding to and reconstructing educational policy texts. In reality, policy texts always and inevitably comprise incomplete specifications for action (Ball 1994) which leave scope for interpretation and choice. Indeed Tyack and Cuban (1995) argue that they should be regarded simply as 'hypotheses', inevitably subject to alteration within the context of a real school. Whilst sweeping legislative changes such as those enacted through the Education Reform Act of 1988 may substantially alter the structural frameworks within which teachers work, such external imperatives are inevitably mediated through human agency and the eventual outcomes depend upon the accumulation of choices and actions taken by individual teachers on a day-to-day basis in their schools and classrooms (Halford and Leonard 1999; Helsby 1999). This is particularly so in organizations such as schools where work cannot be specified, organized and monitored in the same ways as in a telephone-marketing call centre. Neither schools nor education systems are 'tight-coupled', which means that things do not turn out uniformly in the ways that policy-makers and planners intended (Fullan 1999).

Finally, the problems of applying the concepts of 'professionalism' and 'autonomy' to teachers' work are accompanied by a distinct lack of clarity in policy and other discourses about the nature of the 'curriculum' over which they may or may not exercise control. Indeed, many popular discussions of the school curriculum tend to employ a somewhat reductionist view by effectively equating it with the collection of subjects that is taught in schools. In reality, however, there are several aspects of curriculum that are relevant to any consideration of teacher autonomy or professionalism. Most notable amongst these are the following:

- *curriculum content:* this describes or specifies what is to be taught to young people and is frequently expressed in terms of subject titles and associated bodies of knowledge;
- *curriculum method:* this refers to the way in which the content is taught, that is to say the pedagogy;
- *curriculum form:* this describes the timetabled organization of the teaching (for example in subject-specific or cross-curricular units, in blocks of time or on a regular 'drip-feed' basis);
- *curriculum assessment:* this indicates what aspects of learning are formally tested and valued.

Since a fourfold curriculum incorporates particular choices about disputed educational goals and practices, it is a social artefact that is defined and negotiated in various ways at all levels of the education system and inevitably involves political and ideological contestation (Goodson 1994). At the level of the state, and particularly through the 1988 Education Reform Act and associated documentation, attempted definitions focused almost exclusively on the details of curriculum content and associated assessment systems, with curriculum form and curriculum method left to the discretion of individual schools and teachers. Indeed their discretion over such matters as curriculum organization, pedagogy, choice of materials, selection of content (within the bounds of government prescription) and use of textbooks was made quite explicit in some of the official publications produced both before and immediately after the passing of the Education Reform Act (ERA) (DES 1987; 1989). Thus, whilst teachers' autonomy over some aspects of the curriculum appeared to be reduced by the legislation, that over other aspects was formally confirmed for the first time.

As already indicated, however, there is no automatic progression from the intended outcomes of specific policies to the actual outcomes in practice: the 'planned' curriculum as articulated in formal discourses and documentation is generally very different from the 'delivered' curriculum as it is reconstructed by teachers in their own classrooms (and, indeed, different again from what is actually experienced and 'received' by individual students). Accordingly any consideration of the impact of educational reforms must look beyond the formal policy changes to the way in which these are perceived and incorporated into existing practice in schools. This chapter will draw upon evidence from secondary school teachers in the early years of National Curriculum implementation to examine recent changes in curriculum content, method, form and assessment. It will also consider the implications for teachers' sense of control and of professionalism.

## CURRICULUM CHANGE AND TEACHER PROFESSIONALISM

Evidence of teachers' views of curriculum change will be drawn from two major data-sets. The first study was undertaken between 1991 and 1993 as part of the Lancaster TVEI Evaluation Programme, which was directed by Gill Helsby and Murray Saunders. This involved a series of one-to-one semi-structured interviews with some 200 secondary school teachers in two local education authorities (LEAs) and also a survey targeted at all secondary teachers in three LEAs, which elicited over 2000 completed questionnaires. The second set of data comes from the PCT study which is summarized in the Appendix. In addition, some illustrative data are drawn from a more diverse series of teacher interviews conducted by Gill Helsby in 1997–8.

### Curriculum content

The first attempt in recent years to exert central control over the content of the school curriculum came in November 1982 with the surprise announcement of a new Technical and Vocational Education Initiative (TVEI) for 14–18-year-olds, which was to be piloted in the following academic year. The declared aims of the initiative were to stimulate technical and vocational education, to help young people prepare for the world of work and to develop their adaptability and willingness to learn in the face of fast-changing occupational requirements. The scheme was to be administered through a new process of 'categorical funding', whereby LEAs and schools were invited to bid for financial support for development work that met certain pre-specified criteria: those that were funded would subsequently be evaluated for compliance with the initial proposals.

Despite the outraged claims of many educationalists that this represented unwarranted state interference in professional matters, the broadness of the TVEI criteria that eventually emerged, coupled with the lure of additional funding at a time of economic cutbacks, persuaded many to seek involvement in the initiative, and indeed by 1987 all LEAs had launched pilot or preparatory TVEI schemes. Earlier fears that the content of the school curriculum would be dominated by narrow vocational concerns proved unfounded, as the lack of any clear curriculum blueprint, the encouragement of experimentation and the additional resources for staff and curriculum development combined to ensure that TVEI became a truly *educational* initiative, focusing particularly upon the development of new pedagogies (Gleeson 1987; Moore 1990). Indeed, there were claims that TVEI had been 'hi-jacked' by teachers (Harland 1987).

The 1988 ERA, which incorporated the second major attempt to achieve central control of curriculum content, adopted very different approaches. Instead of the open-ended vocational and pedagogic emphases of TVEI, the National Curriculum was firmly based upon a reaffirmation of the importance of traditional school subjects, whose content was to be prescribed through detailed 'programmes of study' and 'attainment targets' for each of the four Key Stages from age five to sixteen. Instead of voluntary participation and categorical funding, National Curriculum implementation was made compulsory in all state schools through legislation and offered few additional resources. Finally, whilst TVEI had openly encouraged diversity and experimentation, schools were to be monitored for conformity with National Curriculum requirements, initially by LEA advisers and subsequently by the new and privatized national inspection body, the Office for Standards in Education (Ofsted).

Although the sudden imposition of a detailed and compulsory national curriculum flew in the face of existing customs and conventions, it is important to distinguish between its earlier and subsequent manifestations. Despite the initial anger at the lack of consultation with teachers over curriculum content, the first detailed versions of the National Curriculum which emerged did represent a form of political compromise (Ball 1994). Prominent educationalists were actively involved both in the working parties appointed to develop the detailed subject specifications and in the national bodies, namely the National Curriculum Council and the Secondary Examinations and Assessment Council, which had oversight of the curriculum and of the formal assessment systems respectively. Vigorous internal debate and, in most cases, public consultation resulted in a series of recommendations that sought to reconcile conflicting views and build upon existing best practice. In the early 1990s, however, after John Major had succeeded Margaret Thatcher as prime minister, there was an increasing tendency for ministers to overturn such recommendations and to substitute their own preferences and prejudices. Largely isolated from the reviled 'educational establishment' and under the strong influence of cultural restorationists, they began to create a 'curriculum of the dead' (Ball 1994), based upon the transmission of traditional knowledge and the testing of factual recall.

As Watkins (1993, p. 82) points out, it is not unusual in a democracy for an education minister to have the power to determine the school curriculum, but it is generally expected that this power 'should be exercised over broad areas of policy leaving the details to professional advisers and should be exercised with restraint'. This was certainly not the case in the early 1990s, when the government became 'increasingly active in the detailed organisation of what [was] happening on the ground' (Bolton 1993, p. 6), despite the claim that there was 'no clarity ... about the Government's vision for the public education service of this country' (p. 9) and that 'the formal channels of advice about education to the Government appear to be muzzled ... or packed with people likely to say whatever the Government wants to hear' (p. 15). Accordingly decisions often appeared arbitrary, whilst lack of consultation and subsequent changes to earlier decisions created considerable confusion amongst teachers about the general aims and direction of the reforms. As Lawton (1993) points out, the national curriculum that emerged was bureaucratic rather than professional and flew in the face of current knowledge about successful curriculum change. Professional concerns and beliefs were ignored in favour of top-down prescription and teachers were 'treated as hirelings to be given instructions rather than as professionals to be involved at all stages and at all levels' (Lawton 1993, p. 66), leaving them feeling 'deskilled and demoralised' (p. 65).

This sense of demoralization was certainly confirmed by some of the secondary school teachers approached in the early 1990s, as shown by these comments from a 1992–3 survey:

> There has been a major change nearly every year. It is time that changes were thought out before being introduced. Morale is very low. My teaching has suffered. I have little interest in the job.

> I feel despair at all the changes – they could not all be implemented properly even if staff and pupils were there twenty-four hours a day.

> No time for consolidation ... feeling of shifting sands, never quite in control of any one aspect any more.

Some teachers did indeed express strong resentment at being excluded from curriculum decision-making in favour of outsiders:

> There's been some bitterness because it's not been decided upon by teachers .... It's the idea of being advised by non-professionals trying to tell you what your job is.
>
> (1993 interview)

> We are the experts, the people who've done the geography degrees, who've been trained to teach geography, who are up to date with it, and yet we're told we're wrong.
>
> (1994 interview)

Two history teachers, interviewed in 1994, directly linked this imposed and extensive external prescription with a decline in their sense of professionalism and a reduction in their classroom autonomy:

> Government interference in history has undermined professionalism. I'm no longer allowed to teach what I've been taught, I have to teach what's been set for me.

> Teachers are finding things forced upon them so they can't use their professional judgement any more ... you can't expand on a subject if the kids are responding or move on if they're not.

Frequently there were differences in response according to subject area. Thus many of the maths teachers interviewed were much less worried by the prescribed content of the National Curriculum, arguing that 'maths is maths' and that the subject content had remained relatively unchanged over the period of the reforms (Saunders and Warburton 1997). Indeed one head of maths interviewed in 1996 believed that teacher professionalism had actually been enhanced because the absence of a National Curriculum textbook had encouraged more collaborative approaches, saying that 'I think that maths teachers talk more about maths now than they ever used to.'

A number of English teachers appeared much less happy with the prescribed content of the National Curriculum, particularly since the heavy emphasis upon the study of 'classic' texts often ran counter to the more progressive and student-centred approaches that had been developed earlier:

I feel very angry about what they've done to English ... we'd honed it to perfection, it was wonderful and then they just threw it all in the air, changed it for no particular reason.
(1994 interview)

We do need to equip them more for life, and not have so much Shakespeare and Dickens, the balance is all wrong .... In English, we used to talk about anything and everything, but there's no time to do that any more, because of all the things you have to do and tick off.
(1997 interview)

Some science teachers also regarded the National Curriculum as a retrograde step:

The advent of GCSE was a major change for good. NEA Modular Science improved on that. New National Curriculum KS4 courses in science have negated that progress, returning pupils to the days of content overload and intellectual demands far beyond the capacities of most 15–16-year-olds.   (1992–3 survey)

Many were particularly exercised by the constant changes in the requirements. Within a year, the considerable amount of work initially invested by teachers in developing new National Curriculum courses was made redundant by the revised orders, leading to considerable resentment and demoralization:

Much time wasted with National Curriculum science [by] changes made in attainment targets, preparation work of high quality largely discarded and money wasted on purchase of books relating to 17 attainment targets now obsolete. Morale rock bottom.
(1992–3 survey)

Arguably, the greatest degree of imposed curriculum change came in technology, which was made compulsory for all students through the National Curriculum. Technology had started to develop as a subject through TVEI from such formerly disparate areas as woodwork, metalwork, technical drawing, home economics, textiles, art and business studies. Whilst its designation as a core subject was seen by some teachers as enhancing their professional status within their school, it nonetheless placed additional pressures upon them. The unevenness of TVEI developments in technology meant that integration presented a major challenge for some, whilst those imbued in the teaching of traditional craft skills were rapidly forced to come to terms with the new focus upon design. To make matters worse, technology, like science, was subject to major revisions in the original national curriculum requirements:

Technology is the subject that the government had made the most mess of, we haven't had any stability for five or six years, neither teachers nor children know what's going on.
(1994 interview)

The extent and duration of these imposed changes had an adverse impact upon many teachers, sapping their confidence and leaving them feeling deskilled. The following comments are taken from interviews with technology teachers in 1995:

A lot of us have seen our strengths totally worn away and feel very, very vulnerable. I knew what I was doing, I knew what I could do, I was strong in this area, I did professional training in this area. They've taken that away from me ... I don't feel that any more.

Technology has changed dramatically over the last two or three years .... Being only two or three weeks ahead of the children tends to undermine confidence.

Keeping abreast of our own subject and the changes in our subjects which are going on ... it frightens us, I think, well, it frightens me anyway, because I think we're not too sure what we're doing ... I don't feel as confident as I used to be in some areas.

However, the last respondent, a female home economics teacher, also claimed later in the same interview that the introduction of the National Curriculum had had some beneficial effects:

> I think in the long run it's done us good, because we've had to rethink, we've had to think about our work.

This view was echoed by a male technology teacher, also interviewed in 1995:

> The National Curriculum gives us a discipline we didn't have before. It made us focus more on our philosophy and what we're about.

Such positive comments generally occurred in departments with a strongly collaborative culture. Indeed in at least two cases the need to develop courses to meet National Curriculum requirements had actually strengthened collaboration within a technology department:

> Initially, we wondered how we would do the National Curriculum. This brought us closer together – in some schools it drove teachers further apart! We asked ourselves what we could do together and how we could make it work ... we knew that the only way forward was to come together as a group, we knew our strengths and weaknesses and we've broken down the barriers. (1996 interview)

Another teacher, interviewed in 1994, spoke of the reassurance and enhanced confidence that came from working closely with colleagues:

> Collaborative meetings do help generally, the team feeling helps to generate loyalty, helps to generate confidence in so much as all the staff are doing the same thing, you don't feel out on a limb ... you don't feel you're being forced into doing things which you don't understand. (1994 interview)

Such feelings point towards the possibility of teachers regrouping to assert greater control of the curriculum, a possibility that increased over time as teachers became more familiar with the requirements:

> I think we now feel more comfortable with the content, slightly more comfortable with the assessment and therefore ... not as straitjacketed, that we must do it like this, by the book. (1995 interview)

This trend was given further support in some subject areas by the decision to abandon the use of SATs and, for all subjects, by the reductions in prescribed content that emerged as a result of the Dearing Review (1993), although opinions did vary over the extent to which this represented a meaningful reduction and many doubted that the promised period of stability would materialize. Increasingly over time, however, there was a sense of teachers recovering from their initial dismay and confusion over the imposition of the National Curriculum, of coming to terms with its demands and of assuming responsibility for its teaching. Thus curriculum content simply ceased to be the major issue for many teachers in terms of their sense of professionalism.

**Curriculum method**

Whilst primary education in England had long been characterized by a strong rhetoric of progressive and pupil-centred pedagogies, particularly in the wake of the Plowden Report (CACE 1967), secondary schools had tended, by and large, to emphasize teachers' subject knowledge over methodological expertise, which was largely taken for granted and therefore ignored. Indeed, the potential freedom associated with the period of 'legitimated professionalism' (Grace 1987) was rarely exploited to develop new and innovative pedagogies in the secondary sector. TVEI, however, explicitly encouraged and celebrated the adoption of 'alternative' approaches to teaching and learning, which were characterized as being 'active', 'flexible', 'student-centred' and 'experiential' – indeed, the rhetoric associated with TVEI often matched that of primary schools. Whilst clear evidence of the *extent* of any changes is elusive, it is certain that many teachers involved in TVEI pilot schemes were offered substantial inducements to experiment – smaller classes, additional non-contact time, teaching resources and other forms of support – and that many believed that they had indeed made some changes in their teaching methods, a view also supported by many of their students (Hinckley 1987).

Even before TVEI could be extended to all schools, however, the announcement of the National Curriculum in 1987 tended to divert attention away from curriculum method and towards the new content. At about the same time, the loss of pilot funding and the vastly reduced levels of support for TVEI extension put an abrupt end to the provision of smaller classes, generous resources and teaching support. Certainly, the National Curriculum regulations, far from specifying any particular pedagogy, explicitly left this to the professional judgement of teachers. In practice, however, by 1991–3 those who had been involved in TVEI pilots were faced with the option of trying to maintain, in much less favourable circumstances, any innovative approaches that they might have developed or of abandoning them, whilst those not yet involved saw few inducements to experiment. Despite some official views noticed in Chapter 4 that pedagogy remained in teachers' control, both groups of teachers found that they were practically constrained by the challenge of accommodating new content in a crowded curriculum.

Amongst the teachers interviewed as part of the TVEI study in 1991–3, there was a degree of agreement both about the importance of pedagogy to teacher professionalism and about the potential usefulness of a secure curriculum framework within which it could be developed:

> If I was told exactly what to do when I went into my classroom during every lesson, that would impinge on my professionalism ... but [the National Curriculum] hasn't done that and it hasn't actually changed my feelings of professionalism in any sense whatsoever, which I think has more to do with the way that you actually do the job than with whether I'm ever allowed a decision about whether to teach Pythagoras or not.

> I think I understand what the curriculum wants and therefore I feel able to make a positive contribution to what's taught.

> In terms of improving the quality of it ... if people know what they're doing, that's a good starting point.

However, a maths teacher found that the potential scope for pedagogical development was, in practice, compromised by other constraints:

> You could argue that, as long as I know what I've got to teach definitely, that could give me the freedom to teach it how I think. But I don't really feel that that's what's happening in practice ... I think pressures of time, lack of time are becoming more noticeable all the time so ... I've tended to stick with what they know and what they can cope with, rather than having the time to set up something very innovative and different.

Similarly, the sheer amount of content that had to be covered in the early years of ERA was seen as inhibiting certain teaching methods:

> It's difficult to develop a variety of teaching and learning styles and get through the content of the National Curriculum. (comment from teacher survey, 1992–3)

> When the National Curriculum first came in, some of the more experiential ways of learning that might have taken a bit longer disappeared almost overnight, as people were struggling to get to grips with the National Curriculum. It all went back to being very content-led. (1997 interview)

The whole notion of developing and improving pedagogy was also threatened by the pressures of meeting external demands and of working with reduced resources:

> I feel under great pressure to deal with all the initiatives and form-filling involved in so many of the changes in education. Worst of all I feel that much of my energy is being diverted from my classroom teaching. (comment from teacher survey, 1992–3)

> you've got increased class size ... we're teaching a slightly heavier timetable and, you know, that has an adverse effect I think on the quality of your teaching. (1996 interview)

On the positive side, some teachers felt that growing familiarity with National Curriculum requirements and, in some cases, the decision to abandon SATs were offering new opportunities to review teaching methods, as indicated by these comments from teacher interviews in 1995:

> We seem to have got an overview of it ... we now feel that we can start looking at what I call styles of learning. We can go back and do more of the role play, the project work.

> The fact that SATs have gone off the horizon means we can actually start to look at what we teach and how we teach it without having to teach for the exam.

However, and despite emergent myths of teacher control of pedagogy, there are indications that the British government – and others – may be appreciating that its enhanced control of curriculum content needs to be complemented by greater control of other aspects of curriculum, such as pedagogy. Arguably, it is becoming the terrain on which curriculum control will be contested and teacher professionalism redefined in the future.

**Curriculum form**

The ways in which the school curriculum is organized can also have important implications for teachers' work and cultures, as well as for their pedagogy. In particular, the arrangement and ordering of subject content, the extent to which the timetable is dominated by subject-specific or cross-curricular priorities and the way in which teaching time is divided, can have significant effects upon teachers' perceptions and practices. Indeed, in the 1992–3 survey of 2010 teachers, major changes in curriculum structure were reported by a greater proportion of respondents (68.9 per cent) compared to either changes in content (51.6 per cent) or changes in methodology (58.1 per cent).

Although it is discussed less frequently than either curriculum content or method, control of curriculum form is important in shaping the level of autonomy enjoyed by both teachers and students. Of particular relevance here are the concepts of 'classification' and 'framing', which Bernstein developed and applied to the various 'message systems' of the curriculum:

> Classification ... refers to the degree of boundary maintenance between contents ... frame refers to the degree of control teacher and pupil possess over the selection, organization and pacing of the knowledge transmitted and received in the pedagogical relationship.
> (Bernstein 1971, pp. 49–50)

According to Bernstein, strong classification tends to vest authority in élite subject groups in universities and to limit teacher control of what is taught, whilst strong framing reduces the autonomy of both teachers and learners within the educational process. Variations in the strength of classification or framing, therefore, are associated with disturbances in existing patterns of authority, leading to 'changes in the structure and distribution of power and in principles of control' (p. 63).

In retrospect, it is clear that the curriculum development work undertaken in many of the TVEI pilot projects had a significant impact upon both classification and framing. A range of new, integrated courses was developed which broke away from the authority of traditional subject hierarchies and emphasized the development and practical application of skills as much as the acquisition of fixed bodies of knowledge. Teachers from different subject areas were centrally involved in the development of these new courses, which relied heavily upon internal assessment, and students were given a degree of choice over content and learning methods. In many cases, changes were made to the school timetable to allow longer blocks of time that would accommodate or facilitate experiential and out-of-school learning. There was also an emphasis upon the cross-curricular development of students' personal and interpersonal skills and expanded provision for careers, health, work-related, economic, civic and personal and social education in many schools. Thus, the boundaries between subjects were considerably weakened whilst both teachers and students were able to exert more control over curriculum content, method and assessment. In other words, the strength of both classification and framing were significantly reduced.

By contrast, and despite official avowals that matters of curriculum organization should be left to the discretion of individual schools (DES 1987; 1989), the introduction of the National Curriculum tended, in practice, to strengthen both classification and framing. This did not occur simply because the National Curriculum was described in terms of a collection of traditional subjects with prescribed content, but also because of the way that the initiative was introduced and managed. For example, the fact that each of the official working groups charged with drawing up the detailed curricular specifications for each National Curriculum subject worked quite separately from each other, with no overarching vision or common conception of key elements such as 'profile components' or 'attainment targets', coupled with the staggered introduction of different National Curriculum subjects into schools, made it virtually impossible, in practical terms, to maintain strong cross-curricular links. This problem was exacerbated at institutional level by the pressures associated with the rapid development of new and different courses in each subject area, which greatly increased teachers' workloads and tended to reinforce traditional 'balkanized' cultures (Hargreaves 1992; Reay 1998). The following comments, taken from teacher interviews in 1992, are fairly typical:

> We talked about links with other departments ... but we just haven't had the time to liaise
> – and the National Curriculum Working Parties never liaise!

> We tried to identify overlaps, but as more and more of the National Curriculum is coming on stream, departments are handing things back to us . . . the National Curriculum pushes people back into departments.

Although the National Curriculum Council belatedly developed suggestions for a number of cross-curricular 'dimensions', 'skills' and 'themes' that were to be incorporated into the school curriculum (NCC 1989), the fact that they were non-statutory, their generally low status compared to recognized 'subjects', an overall lack of resources and heavy workloads in schools all combined to ensure that they were usually either ignored or marginalized. Additionally, the newly tightened assessment requirements focused on individual subjects, and not on cross-curricular achievements:

> Cross-curricular themes have very low priority – schools have to put in enormous effort just to get the main courses up and running, and this has top priority. Cross-curricular things tend to take more organization than things that happen in one department.
>                                                                                         (1993 interview)

> It's hard to break the autonomy of individual subject departments because of the subject-specific accreditation.                                                          (1993 interview)

A comment from a 1997 interview with a teacher who had formerly been closely involved in TVEI developments pointed towards the potentially isolating effects of this reversion to a subject-specific emphasis:

> The cross-curricular nature of the curriculum has gone and that's sad . . . now everyone's gone back in their little boxes . . . we've gone back to the hierarchy of subjects.

At the same time, the 1944 prescription of religious education, added to the 1988 requirement that all secondary school students should study ten National Curriculum subjects, each with a large amount of prescribed content, encouraged a more fragmented timetable with a regular 'drip-feed' approach to teaching. At the turn of the century, that approach is reinforced with the addition of information and communication technology, and citizenship, as identifiable subjects. The use of longer blocks of time to support experiential learning was largely abandoned, and teachers used to those longer blocks were obliged to adjust their pedagogical approaches to shorter units of contact time. At the same time, increasing resource constraints meant that many were given both heavier teaching loads and larger classes.

Thus it could be argued that some of the structural and organizational changes that were encouraged, if not ordained, by National Curriculum requirements had a constraining effect upon the autonomy of many teachers. Not only did the 'reforms' inhibit cross-curricular working and expose teachers once again to the 'hierarchy of subjects', but the heavy content load and, in some cases, shorter teaching periods also combined to limit the possibilities for pedagogical experimentation. Some developments may ease this curriculum corset, developments such as some reductions in the content coverage required in each subject; such as the greater possibilities for getting dispensation from National Curriculum requirements at Key Stage 4; and the impact of the moderately revised National Curriculum that will operate late in the year 2000. However, it remains to be seen how these developments will be worked through and how they will interact with other changes to which we have referred (such as the introduction of a new subject, 'citizenship') that may further constrain the form of the curriculum.

**Curriculum assessment**

Commonly used terms such as 'assessment-led curriculum' and 'teaching to the test' are indicative of the potential importance of assessment systems in determining the shape of the school curriculum and the nature of teachers' work. The widespread abandonment of the eleven-plus examination, for example, was often associated with innovation and curriculum development in primary schools. Conversely, the need for most secondary school students to gain nationally recognized qualifications at the age of sixteen has meant that the requirements of university-based examining boards placed significant constraints upon teachers' classroom autonomy during the so-called 'golden age' of legitimated professionalism and beyond. Although these constraints were briefly relaxed during the early years of TVEI pilots, when the examining boards validated a range of new, teacher-developed courses that relied largely or wholly on internal assessment, this freedom was once more curtailed by the emphasis upon national testing that was reintroduced with the National Curriculum.

As in the case of curriculum content, it is necessary to distinguish between earlier and later versions of the National Curriculum assessment requirements. The earlier versions, symbolized by the report of the Task Group on Assessment and Testing (TGAT 1987) and officially endorsed in subsequent government guidance (DES 1989), were based upon a combination of teacher assessment and external testing, were rooted in classroom practice and had strong diagnostic and formative intentions. Later versions, however, increasingly sidelined formative and teacher assessment and instead emphasized simple, summative judgements through the use of externally marked pen-and-paper tests. A former senior HMI, interviewed in 1996 as part of the PCT study, believed that these changes in assessment were far more damaging to teacher professionalism than the prescription of curriculum content:

> I think that [control of assessment] is absolutely crucial to the notion of the professionalism of the teacher. Because if they're not trusted to carry out assessment, then their professionalism is really knocked for six, because their whole judgement is then questioned.

Certainly some of the teachers interviewed expressed a degree of resentment at the current lack of trust in their judgement:

> You're much more accountable now ... justifying yourself, what you've done, why you've given that child A or B or whatever. Where before you could just say, 'Well, that's my judgement of them', but now you've got to have evidence.          (1996 interview)

> One cannot teach for testing, and our professional judgement is so doubted that record-keeping to justify known levels of achievement is deforesting the planet. (1992–3 survey)

However, the new emphasis upon national testing and, in particular, the publication of comparative 'league tables' of assessment results were also having wider effects upon teachers and upon the school curriculum. On the one hand, it was suggested that this imposed fresh constraints upon pedagogy:

> National Curriculum assessment means that you are teaching more to the test or exam, there's a loss of flexibility. The investigative approach in science is laid down in a particular way in the National Curriculum ... it's become so rigid and formalized. (1993 interview)

> Because schools are now driven by results, you teach to get the results, so they can't answer the interesting questions ... teachers feel they have to finish this today, they need to cover the curriculum.                          (deputy headteacher interview, 1997)

On the other hand, it was seen as influencing teacher thinking about curriculum content and posing a threat to some educationally important but formally unassessed areas of the curriculum:

> There should be personal and social education in the curriculum, but I know of some teachers who are thinking, 'Well, that doesn't actually appear in the league tables. If they do more science or they do more maths, that actually appears in the league tables.'
>
> (1995 interview)

Perhaps even more significantly, it was suggested that the increased competition generated by the league tables was having an adverse effect upon teacher collaboration both within and between schools:

> Not everyone likes working in teams together, especially if you're looking at who gets what grades. The pressures to get results are up and to nail people who are not getting the grades. (1997 interview)

> I do not agree with these league tables at all, I do not agree with the publishing of school results, because that just sets up competition ... when we should be supporting and encouraging each other and helping each other along. It's dividing the profession right down the middle. (1995 interview)

This idea of a fragmented occupational group was also supported by another teacher, who claimed that the increased isolation served to diminish her own sense of professionalism:

> It's difficult to see other staff ... there's no forum for ideas or concerns to be expressed, and that contributes to this feeling of not being professionals: you're just an isolated body in a classroom. (1995 interview)

Finally, the important consequences of the new assessment and reporting arrangements described above are, in many ways, exacerbated by other recent educational reforms that may combine to make teachers' work more difficult:

> SATs, the publication of results, a tight inspectorate and the market are all working on us, the pressures are getting inexorably worse. (1997 interview)

## CURRICULUM CHANGE AND TEACHER PROFESSIONALISM

It is clear that, directly or indirectly, the 1988 ERA and related legislation resulted in some very significant structural changes to all four aspects of the school curriculum considered above. It is equally clear from the evidence above, however, that curriculum practice is variable, both between schools and over time, and that the notion of 'control' of the school curriculum is subject to constant contestation and reinterpretation at all levels. Central policy-makers may see their detailed policy texts as predictors of curricular reality, but in fact they are starting points for change and remain dependent upon schools, departments and teachers to translate their suggested courses of action into curricular practice. Moreover, the fact that teachers must accommodate any new demands within existing practice and relationships automatically necessitates a degree of compromise between continuity and change: as Tyack and Cuban (1995, p. 82) point out, 'Policymakers may ignore the "pedagogical past," but teachers and students cannot.' Within the field of research into school effectiveness and school improvement a similar point is being recognized, namely that contingencies are important in shaping schools' departments' and teachers' responses to calls for educational improvement (Gewirtz 1998; Turner and Bolam 1998; Gray *et al.* 1999).

The introduction of the National Curriculum was, however, quite distinct from the curricular policies reviewed in Part 1 because of the multiple and overt attempts to ensure hierarchical control and to tighten the traditionally 'loosely-coupled' English education system. An increasingly sophisticated understanding of curriculum that led policy-makers to appreciate that curriculum is more than content lay behind a series of actions that brought about a far more tightly coupled curriculum specification for the nation's schools. Not only was curriculum content prescribed in unprecedented detail and made compulsory through legislation, but assessment systems were also dictated centrally, with teachers' judgements increasingly marginalized. Given the known impact of tight assessment systems upon curriculum content, this dual strategy could in itself be seen as unnecessary overkill. However, further steps were also taken in an attempt to ensure teacher compliance with central policies. First, schools were to be inspected for conformity with National Curriculum requirements and, second, comparative tables of assessment results were to be made public at a time when schools were being forced to compete for pupils in order to maximize their funding.

Teachers reacted to these changes in varied ways and, because of the staggered introduction of National Curriculum subjects, different groups were galvanized at different times during the early years of implementation. Bowe *et al.* (1992), in an initial study of this period, point towards great variations in response between teachers, between subject departments and between schools, depending on whether they chose to regard policy texts as instructions for action, with little scope for deviation and creativity, or as suggested strategies, to be interpreted and adapted. A key factor in such choices is the level of 'professional confidence' (Helsby 1995): where confidence is high, teachers and communities of teachers (such as departments or schools) are more likely to adopt an interpretative role, whilst low levels of confidence render them more amenable to external instruction and manipulation.

There is a good deal to suggest that levels of individual and collective professional confidence were adversely affected by the effects of the 1988 ERA, particularly in the early stages (see, for example, Helsby and McCulloch 1997; Woods and Jeffrey 1997). The destabilizing effects of constant change, repeated exposure to public 'discourses of derision' (Ball 1990), increasing isolation and the reassertion of central curriculum prescription all served to demoralize many teachers, who for some time felt themselves effectively deskilled. Others, however, maintained the capacity to adopt a more proactive role with regard to the reforms and, as shown in some of the examples above, were able to work with colleagues and approach the changes as opportunities for professional learning and growth. As time went by, growing familiarity with National Curriculum requirements and experience of successfully developing and employing new skills served once more to enhance teachers' confidence and to allow them increasingly to find spaces in which to exercise their professional judgement.

As well as shifts in teachers' attitudes and approaches, there have also been significant changes to the central policy texts themselves over time. Some of these changes have been described above in terms of earlier or later versions of the National Curriculum, but there have also been other modifications that have occurred as a result of teachers' responses to policies or of problems encountered during their realization in practice. For example, there was a successful teacher boycott of SATs in 1993, whilst the combination of evident curriculum overload and complex assessment systems led to the Dearing review of the National Curriculum and its assessment. The subsequent recommendations resulted in reductions in the prescribed content of the programmes of study, in the number of attainment targets and in the number of statements of attainment. However, what was described as '[t]his increased trust in teachers' was to be 'matched by accountability to parents and society, including that from simple tests in core subjects' (Dearing 1993, p. 25). Whilst the simplification of national tests, their restriction to core subjects and external marking all served to ease teachers' workloads, they also introduced a form of 'high stakes' assessment that had implications both for curricular planning and for the exercise of professional judgement by teachers. And although the revision of the curriculum for the year 2000 was deliberately an incremental one whose headline feature was the introduction of compulsory lessons in 'citizenship', this self-restraint may be viewed as the latest in a series of incremental changes since 1995, when five years of stasis were promised. Indeed, only days after the revised curriculum framework was announced in the summer of 1999, a new policy announcement said that a government priority would be to improve the quality of sex education in schools for adolescents.

Thus, the English school curriculum remains an arena of contestation in which different groups struggle to impose their own values, beliefs and interpretations of the nature of education and of teachers' proper role within it. As political theories, discourses and myths move in and out of fashion, and as politicians come and go, the patterns of policy-making will also continue to change. Equally, as teachers gain or lose confidence, they will play a more or less assertive role in policy realization and are likely to become more or less 'professional'. It is not possible here to unpick all the strands of teacher professionalism and examine how they have been differently woven over the past fifteen years. However, it is possible to select one and to examine it closely so as to get a more detailed idea of how structural changes have reacted with teacher professionalism. Given that change depends upon learning, we chose to examine teachers' professional development as one – but only as one – indicator of the ways in which changes to structures and discourses over the past fifteen years have impacted upon teachers' professional standing. That is the subject of the next chapter.

# Chapter 6

# Teachers' Professional Development

It is widely believed that the wealth of industrialized nations does not rest upon their supplies of raw materials and on their traditional manufacturing industries. The new orthodoxy is that wealth will increasingly depend upon the knowledge, skills and entrepreneurship of their citizens. Given that knowledge and skills quickly date, it follows that a nation will be competitive in some proportion to the degree that its people continually update their knowledge and skills. Nowhere is this more true than in the education sector, because if teachers are to promote world-class standards in world-class schools, they need to be continually developing their own expectations, knowledge and skills. Furthermore, teachers need to extend their repertoires as their careers develop and they take on new responsibilities.

Two questions arise from this scenario. The first is what sort of learning teachers ought to experience – should it be directed to improving their technical skills at delivering curricula devised by others, or should it be professional learning, encouraging creativity, reflection and consideration of the best forms of education for the different needs of the children they teach? Bottery and Wright (1996) and Bottery (1998) have argued that teachers' continued learning ought to be professional in that a crucial element of professionalism is giving priority to the needs of clients. That involves thinking about the goals, place and purposes of education provision and forming a view of teachers' place in society. We shall suggest that in-service provision (INSET) has recently been dominated by issues to do with putting government policies into place in classrooms.

The second question relates to the form of professional development. The usual assumption is that professional development opportunities should be provided for teachers. While that does happen (although these opportunities have tended to dwell on implementation issues), there are other ways in which learning and professional learning take place. We shall argue that these alternative ways of learning are important and that they are best sustained by good departmental leadership. In a very important sense, the subject department in school is the centre of continued professional learning. The question therefore becomes one of how 'learning departments' can be embedded in the educational system. This is a vision of professional learning and development that is in sharp contrast to the approach to it embodied in the English Green Paper on new professionalism (DfEE 1998), with its reliance on reform of formal, course-based professional development.

## CHANGE, OBSOLESCENCE AND PROFESSIONAL LEARNING

Teachers' work changes in the natural, normal course of their careers – they change schools, work with new colleagues, take on fresh responsibilities, and engage with children from different social and educational backgrounds. Challenges such as these are frequently spurs to learning (Smylie 1995). In the past that learning was, to a considerable extent, under the teacher's control. Teachers chose to seek promotion, often chose to take on new responsibilities and tended to have a say in whether they would engage in curriculum development activities or not (Nias *et al.* 1992). Some opted to put almost all of their energies into classroom-focused issues, acting as 'restricted professionals' in Hoyle's terms (1974). They could direct their professional learning accordingly or, if satisfied with their work, could choose not to engage consciously in any further professional learning. On the other hand, 'extended professionals', who also had interests in general educational issues, policy and school-wide concerns, could choose professional learning activities that would complement their more extensive interests. The picture is of a relatively stable past in which teachers might choose not to be consciously involved in professional learning activities and where those who did take up the opportunities expected to be able to chart their own, personal development route, often by selecting from courses made available by local authorities and higher education institutions.

Chapter 5 described increasing government intervention in schools which we will argue has greatly contributed to professional obsolescence (Willis and Dubin 1990). The next five paragraphs suggest some of the ways in which professional obsolescence has become endemic as a consequence of continued government intervention.

First, these mandated changes, common in Western countries, have affected discourses. Official views have changed about the content, form and organization of the curriculum; about the standing and roles of teachers; and about educational goals and standards. Each of these changes has implications for teachers' beliefs and classroom practices. So, at one point in the past the priority was to master mixed ability teaching, but at another it was to raise the proportion of students getting grades A–C in the GCSE examinations; here history and geography were taught as integrated humanities, while there mathematics was to be seen as a problem-working practical and investigative activity; licensed autonomy gave way to the more tightly licensed, lesser autonomy of National Curriculum prescriptions.

Second, the National Curriculum in England has enlarged the knowledge base needed in teaching. Primary school teachers had to master a substantial set of subjects, issues and concerns. Although secondary school teachers, who tend to be subject specialists, did not have so much new material to master, many did have new learning to do. Mathematics teachers tended to say that 'maths is maths', meaning that they seldom had new content to master. But, for some humanities teachers, the National Curriculum brought new topics and many technology teachers found that the newly defined subject faced them with new topics and obliged them to consider their work within a more complex and integrated disciplinary framework than hitherto.

Third, the knowledge base was not extended simply in terms of content. Probably the most radical learning demands were associated with the need to plan, teach and assess with detailed levels of attainment in mind and with the intention of catering for the different achievements of pupils in any group. The assessment requirements of the National Curriculum, as expressed in the TGAT report (1987), may have been conceptually related to the philosophy behind the familiar GCSE examinations, but they were also different in detail, in their meaning in the context of new topics, and because they were to be regularly applied to all children in Years 7–11.

Moreover, these fresh demands made greater calls on teachers' non-routine decision-making. Guidance on what to do was often seen to be limited, and such guidance as there was still left teachers to make meaning of the innovation in specific circumstances and with reference to specific topics (Fullan 1991). In the past, it was possible to deal with problems by not teaching problematic topics (like the English Reformation or the 'Glorious Revolution' – arguably it was neither – of 1688), or by avoiding troublesome routines (continuing to plan in terms of activities, rather than in terms of the officially preferred learning outcomes). The National Curriculum was intended to shut off those expressions of the 'practicality ethic' and force teachers to make non-routine decisions about problems that could once have been avoided.

Lastly, the Education Reform Act embodied what some saw as utilitarian values in which the production of (often contentious) learning outcomes was privileged over the quality of processes of learning (see Crawford 1996, on the case of the history curriculum). That threatened the identity and professional claims of teachers whose beliefs were that the processes of learning were more important than mastery of any pre-specified learning outcomes associated with a body of knowledge. So, teachers' values and their professional skills were often challenged by the changes.

## THREE ASSUMPTIONS

To put it another way, restricted professionals are now expected to engage with issues that previously attracted only extended professionals, and extended professionals are expected to engage with those issues on terms set out by government agencies. System-wide changes, of which the National Curriculum is but one, have produced the disruption that can provoke learning.

The complex of changes in England in the past fifteen years is so extensive and so well policed (by SATs, appraisal, Ofsted inspections and the operation of quasi-markets, for example) that a non-learning response has scarcely been viable. By and large, teachers have had to change, to a greater or lesser degree. Change involves learning. That is not to say that all teacher learning has been successful, nor that teachers have learned all the things that they needed to in order to conform with the ideals of policy-makers. It is a simple statement that as the great majority of teachers have changed in the face of professional obsolescence, so learning has been involved.

This learning, which is directed to the improvement of children's learning, might be called professional 'development', although this is a term of approbation, a value judgement. For example, it would be tricky to claim that learning how to cut corners

**Table 6.1 Change and learning**

| Response to change prompt (Point 1 is logically derived, while point 2 comes from 1970s literature on the implementation of large-scale curriculum projects. 3 & 4 come from Argyris 1985.) | Substantive learning (Learning about the change itself: for example, gaining a better understanding of the nature of outcomes; of the principles behind outcomes-led curricula; of how to write outcomes.) |
| --- | --- |
| 1. No response needed: it is believed that existing practices and discourses meet what the prompt encourages. Alternatively, prompt is ignored or rejected. | 1. None. |
| 2. Change without change: cosmetic adjustments that indicate compliance without involving a change in practice. | 2. Some incidental learning about the change is possible, although the most likely substantive outcome is no learning. |
| 3. Single-loop change: changes affect ways of doing things within the existing framework of assumptions and discourses. | 3. Single-loop learning. |
| 4. Double-loop change: change extends to assumptions and discourses. | 4. Double-loop learning. |

and minimize the effort of teaching counted as professional 'development', although it would not be impossible, particularly as long hours of working are not necessarily signs of job effectiveness (Campbell and Neill 1994b). Likewise, professional 'development' associated with the National Curriculum could be characterized as exactly the opposite of development, on the grounds that the National Curriculum valued test scores on a narrowly conceived curriculum over child-centred processes of education, which some saw as the quintessence of schooling. Where learner-centred, enquiry-based TVEI curriculum developments had to give ground to more traditional pedagogies, it might be appropriate to query the idea that professional learning has taken place. On that analysis, learning about implementing the National Curriculum would be seen as professional regression.

Table 6.1 is an attempt to draw together different levels of response to change with different forms of learning. So, there are cases of non-response, whether through good reasons ('we're already doing it') or others; there are cases of window dressing; and cases of different levels of substantive learning. What is not shown in the table are the cases where a response to change could be seen by some party or another as an example of professional regression, of professional unlearning. Judging that a change is a step backwards is probably more contentious than assuming that a change marks a development because it runs so much against our deep assumptions that change is progress. Nevertheless, it is worth bearing in mind that some of the changes of the past fifteen years are seen by some as regress, not progress.

Equally, there can be disagreement about the degree to which any development is 'professional' in character. It might be argued that teaching is a profession and that therefore all teacher development is, by definition, 'professional' development. How-ever, there are analyses of teachers' work that claim that teaching is becoming deprofessionalized, deskilled and proletarianized (Ozga 1989; Apple 1993; Hargreaves 1994). These claims are more closely examined in the next chapter. For present purposes it is enough to notice that these analyses suggest that some changes to teachers' work reduce teachers' power to decide on goals and methods and effectively make them technicians following someone else's designs. Consequently, there is a case for saying that teacher development activities that are designed to make them more technically skilled, while removing from them design and moral questions (Sockett 1993) and thereby extending outside control of teachers' work, should not be called 'professional' development. Again, it is beyond the scope of this chapter to explore that important point. For simplicity, it will be assumed that teachers' learning is 'pro-fessional'.

The assumptions that have been noted in this section are:

- Change produces learning
- Learning is developmental, something to be approved of
- Teachers' learning is professional learning

It has also been observed that these assumptions do not always hold good. That should be borne in mind in reading the following analyses, which differ somewhat from the other writing in Part 2. This chapter cites less of the empirical evidence from the TVEI and PCT projects than do the other chapters and is more given over to developing a position about what professional development should – and should not – look like. Helsby and Knight (1997) make more obvious use of those primary PCT project data.

## WHAT ARE PROFESSIONALS TO LEARN?

### Emotional learning

Thought and emotion – cognition and affect – are intertwined. Consequently, effective-ness at work relates to cognitive strength – to levels of understanding, for example – but it is also related to affective factors, especially to motivational factors. Sternberg (1997) in his discussion of intelligence testing claims that IQ, a measure of cognitive ability, has no more than a +0.2 correlation with life success. Cooper and Sawaf (1997) take a similar line, arguing that emotional mastery and sensitivity are more important in work and life generally than is the intelligence that is measured by IQ tests.

The emotions are especially significant in people-working occupations, where many people get their rewards not from their pay as much as from the psychic or intrinsic rewards of work that can be emotionally satisfying. The PCT study provided plenty of examples of the emotional stresses attached to teaching in the early 1990s, but it also confirmed that the job was also a source of fulfilment to most of the teachers we interviewed. Evans (1998) has developed Hertzberg's two-factor theory of motivation to argue that extrinsic factors, such as pay and working conditions, can produce or reduce dissatisfaction, but that it is only intrinsic factors, such as enjoyment, satisfaction, belief in the value of the work, that can produce feelings of fulfilment. This picture is compatible with the analyses of the emotions and teaching in the 1996 special issue of the *Cambridge Journal of Education* and with the work of Andy Hargreaves on the emotions in teaching (Hargreaves 1994; 1998). Teaching can be emotionally hard and even threaten the teacher's self-esteem and sense of identity. Yet, for many teachers it is the psychic rewards, the emotional 'feelgood', that provide the rewards that make teaching a fulfilling experience. Although Hargreaves (1999a) has suggested that these rewards may be less intense and come in different contexts for secondary, as opposed to primary, teachers, it still seems that they are rewards that matter.

One conclusion is that the best professional learning would capitalize upon and consolidate intrinsic motivation, which would suggest that teachers should have some scope to choose what to learn, when and how. That is not possible in times of system-wide change where government imperatives drive professional learning. It is, of course, possible that learning that began under extrinsic duress may prove to be interesting and satisfying, so that it continues for intrinsic reasons. Yet, there must be some concern about the quality of learning and its contribution to teachers' overall morale when the main drivers are extrinsic.

These psychic rewards are typically found in face-to-face work with children in the classroom. However, the work of Campbell and Neill (1994b) has suggested that recent changes to schooling in England have reduced the proportion of time teachers spend teaching children to about 35 per cent of the working week; have increased the priority given to activities that the majority of teachers regard as less fulfilling, such as planning, policy-making and record-keeping; have made more demands on classroom time, often leading to a feeling that it is impossible to get anything done properly; and have reduced the scope for responding to children's expressed needs and interests. Hargreaves (1994) has shown how guilt and shame, which are the dark side of intrinsic motivation, can be compounded by developments such as these. Not only can such changes make it hard for teachers to feel the success that is so important for sustaining intrinsic motivation and personal well-being, they can also be associated with stress and 'burn-out' (Fisher 1994). In the face of constant, mandated change and of threatening accountability procedures, such as Ofsted inspections (Woods and Jeffrey 1998), teachers may learn helplessness (Seligman 1998), believing themselves to be victims who are scarcely able to shape the patterns of their work and to find rewards in it. The ensuing passivity, disillusion and defensiveness, sometimes manifesting themselves as cynicism, obstructiveness or anger, are hardly conducive to good schooling or to professional learning. In such situations, stress and 'burn-out' are more likely (Cooper and Payne 1988) and 'without attention to the emotions, educational reform efforts may ignore and even damage some of the most fundamental aspects of what teachers do' (Hargreaves 1998, p. 850). They may also damage teachers.

So, the day-to-day work of teaching brings emotions forcefully into play – in Lortie's phrase (1975), it is a cathected activity. Golby (1996) showed how three primary school teachers' educational practices were influenced by their emotions (in tandem with their cognitions, of course). He suggested that these emotions led them to be, perhaps, too defensive, too proprietorial and to take an individualist rather than a 'whole school' approach to educational matters. Work in the USA had reached similar conclusions about teacher individualism and collegiality (Jackson 1968; Lortie 1975). Yet, education developments in England, especially the National Curriculum, are premised on the belief that, in the secondary school, curriculum consistency, continuity and progression all depend upon department-wide and whole-school approaches: on collegiality.

Emotions are important in teachers' work and it is possible to influence them in the work context. In other words, it is possible and desirable to see professional development extending to emotional learning. With roots in the humanistic psychology pioneered by Abraham Maslow (for example, 1998) and developed by Carl Rogers (for example, 1983), one theme is that feelings are influential in actions and that they can be changed, thereby making other actions possible (Palmer 1998). For example, in the face of structural changes to the education system, both in Britain and in other Western countries, teachers may feel helpless victims or they may see possibilities for making spaces and colonizing the changes. Others may feel bruised and pessimistic in consequence of their negative experiences of attempts to introduce reforms (Little 1992). The learned helplessness of feeling like a victim saps intrinsic motivation and emotional rewards, substituting the stress of a tension between an ideal and the constrictions of the present. In a study of new university lecturers, Perry *et al.* (1996) found that people like that, who had a locus of external control, felt much less happy than those who had a locus of internal control and felt that they could work creatively within the same structural framework. The social psychologist Martin Seligman has reached similar conclusions and adds the claim that helplessness and optimism, both emotional states, may be learned (1998). Those seeking to reform education would do well to help teachers to see the possibilities for exercising their agency, thereby reducing feelings of helplessness and of victimization.

In a similar vein techniques such as Neuro-Linguistic Programming offer guidance on ways of putting different frames of interpretation around events so that different understandings lead to different feelings and to different actions. In this and other approaches, techniques such as 'helicoptering' (standing back), visioning (imagining an ideal outcome), attending to body posture and body language (relaxing postural tensions), and breathing mindfully (breathing into the bottom as well as into the top of the lungs) can all be used to affect the way events are felt and the consequent reactions. And there is a host of books and tapes on self-esteem, self-image, stress reduction and personal efficacy, all of which aim to change thought and behaviour as feelings and beliefs are worked upon.

This short review of emotional learning and teaching is not presented as a new form of social engineering, a more effective 'colonisation of the affective' (Willmott 1993). The argument is that emotional learning is an important and personal component of professional learning. Nevertheless, none of our respondents alluded to it. There appeared to be no formal provision for it. Yet, that is not to say that there were no opportunities for emotional learning. Where people work collegially, interpersonal skills are called for and emotional intelligence is valuable and may be developed in the daily business of working together. A lot then depends on the quality of team leadership and of working relationships. This idea that the activity system – the main work group – is a site of professional learning is one to which we shall return.

## Cognitive learning

*Values and purposes*

Twenty years ago, in the days of licensed autonomy, it was believed that change would be most effective where teachers could agree on the purposes and goals of the curriculum, thence on its content, on pedagogies and on assessment methods. They might also evaluate and refine curriculum, coming close to the idea of action research. In that setting it was fitting for there to be awareness of the moral dimension of teaching, for educators to ask moral questions about the purposes and functions of the curriculum in relation to different groups of children and in the context of different social interest groups. However, our informants' questionnaire responses provided scant evidence that this view had any place in formal professional development activities. Government mandates had effectively made such matters obsolete. Indeed, it is possible to argue that teaching is being deprofessionalized because teachers' autonomy to design curricula and to determine the goals of education has been limited: design issues have been arrogated to government, with teachers left only to execute others' designs. While a response might observe that since 1995 teachers have had more scope to choose curriculum content, a riposte would point to incipient government control of pedagogy in the shape of the literacy hour that has been enjoined on primary schools.

Yet we did find teachers who, working within the National Curriculum framework, had reflected upon aims, purposes and philosophy, often with their colleagues, and brought their understandings to bear in adapting the National Curriculum to their stances. For example

> Still, you do it your way, to the extent that you're a professional you're not just doing as you're told ... insofar as the syllabuses provide a framework, you still do it your way, you know ... you can do it through Shakespeare to a degree – I'm not being too, sort of, subversive – you can do it through poetry or newspapers but you're teaching the same appreciation of words. (English teacher, PCT pilot interview, 1994)

> I think if a teacher role is to provide a good liberal education through the offices of whatever curriculum he's involved with, then I can't really see what's changed ... I think the changes have been superficial, to be honest. (History teacher, 1995)

> I use my professional judgement in the selection of content. (History teacher, 1995)

Recent North American literature on public and with-profit organizations suggests that it is important that organizations, such as the departments in which these teachers worked and talked, take values issues seriously. It places considerable emphasis on the importance of an organization having clear and understood values that are shared and which pervade all its activities (for example, Badaracco and Ellsworth 1989; Hesselbein *et al.* 1996; Peters 1994). A prime leadership task is to work with followers to articulate a vision and attendant values. A second-order task is to insist on the importance of those values while encouraging people to choose their own ways of manifesting the values in their work. This is sometimes known as simultaneous tight–loose coupling: tight on vision and values, loose about the means by which they are furthered. In this literature the organization that lacks such a moral or values direction is seen as inferior. And what applies to the whole organization applies, perhaps with more force, to the sub-unit, such as the subject department or course team. Leaders and followers both need to learn about the creation of workplace cultures around a sense of purpose and its associated values.

Yet, we heard little about formal in-service provision for departmental management and leadership. We also observed a lack of formal opportunities for teachers to learn to work in teams, to clarify purposes and values, and to develop collegial, non-threatening workplace cultures. In terms of formal provision it can be said that teachers' professional learning is missing a dimension that is seen to be very important by researchers in organization studies.

*Learning about pedagogy and curriculum content*

We know of no research into the way teachers respond to the need to teach new curriculum material, but we do know from research into teachers' planning that content looms largest in their thinking about their lessons. From this we surmise that it is desirable that plenty of support be given to teachers who are mastering new content.

The National Curriculum caused some pedagogic obsolescence. The non-statutory guidance for the subjects of the curriculum often commended ways of promoting learning that were at variance with some established, didactic routines, and some attainment target statements virtually demanded that teachers use a wide pedagogic repertoire. For example, the 1989 mathematics curriculum requires pupils to 'design a task and select appropriate mathematics and resources' (DFE 1989, p. 4); to 'construct simple 2-D and 3-D shapes from given information' (p. 27); and to 'design and use an appropriate observation sheet to collect data' (p. 32). Moreover, teaching had to be directed towards the promotion of national norm-referenced standards (which were expressed in criterion-related terms) and it was to be located within school-wide policies for developing pupil learning in the National Curriculum subjects. Generally, this was new. Given that the government directed subject working groups to draw on best practice in framing the National Curriculum specifications, it can be inferred that they required new learning for many teachers.

The new content and new pedagogic requirements came together in the details of curriculum expectations for each subject, where teachers needed to learn ways of delivering both new and old material to national standards within a heavily loaded timetable.

In the mid-1980s TVEI had also challenged teachers' content knowledge and pedagogies. While it cannot be said that this was always a comfortable process, it could be fulfilling. Certainly, when considering the first wave of TVEI schools, which were well-funded, reasons include:

- good levels of access to INSET courses and other professional development activities, with supply cover for attendance during the school day;
- teacher control of the curriculum within the broad TVEI framework (see Chapter 5);
- adequate resources for TVEI curriculum development;
- time for teachers to plan and to learn from one another.

In contrast, our conversations with teachers in the PCT project intimated that:

- INSET provision, including timetabled on-site meetings, had become more extensive *and* remained quite insufficient to meet the needs created by educational reforms;
- access to courses had been restricted, often being limited to senior staff;
- in-service provision had tended to be very functional, concentrating on the 'nuts and bolts' of delivering the National Curriculum;
- in some cases the quality had been suspect, with claims made that course providers hardly knew that of which they spoke;
- resources to support this new learning had been in short supply, both as a result of cash constraints and because of late publication of materials;
- too much had to be learned and done in too short a time;
- continuing changes in some subjects and increased workloads overall meant that learning was taking place in circumstances in which coping strategies would have been appropriate.

Formal provision to help teachers face the effects of professional obsolescence might be characterized as instrumental and functional – closer to technician education than to professional learning.

## PROFESSIONAL OR TECHNICAL LEARNING?

It could be said that both TVEI and the National Curriculum have contributed to – even caused – the proletarianization of teaching. Within a Marxist sociology, professions are anomalous, being neither capitalist enterprises nor pure wage labour. It has been expected that the anomaly would be regularized as late capitalism, in its recurrent crises, drove professionals into the position of wage labourers. In the process, the work they did would be simplified and routinized, so that complex work done by semi-independent practitioners could now be undertaken by (less-well-paid) technicians doing essentially routine work under the surveillance of bureaucratic management. In such a case professional learning would be displaced by demonstrably cost-effective technicist training.

Indeed, it has proved hard for teachers to create spaces in the National Curriculum where they can do what they judge to be in the learners' best interests, funding has been restricted, time has been compressed, and opportunities for formal learning (through courses and conferences, for example) have been limited and often confined to more senior staff. The inadequacy of formal provision was remarked upon by a senior politician in the governing Conservative party, who was one of our key informants:

> One of the things we are unhappy about at the moment . . . is the lack of opportunities for teachers to express their professionalism by taking advantage of INSET courses.

A senior member of Ofsted was less concerned about the amount of provision but was very anxious about the quality of INSET saying that there was

> five hundred million, if not largely down the drain, it certainly isn't having the impact it should have . . . surely the essence of professionalism is self-reliance, rather than dependency upon some external source of expertise?

Another simply said 'they [teachers] won't get much continuous professional development' and went on to argue that it was therefore imperative that the normal workings of the school promoted continuing, workplace learning. Indeed, the fact that the National Curriculum has in some form been implemented means that professional learning has often taken place (but not always, given the idea of professional regression), even if that learning has not mainly been through the agency of formal in-service programmes. The question is whether that has mainly involved teachers learning to be curriculum operatives, people who 'drive' a standardized and routinized curriculum through the classroom. This is discussed further in Chapter 7. Here, comment is restricted to two observations. One is that teachers have had to learn to work within a much more complex curriculum, which has required new skills of them and, as the example of the new assessment requirements shows, considerable amounts of non-routine judgement. The other is that the teachers in the PCT study frequently said that the autonomy that mattered to them was the autonomy of classroom practice. It was more important for them to be able to decide how to teach than to decide what to teach.

In this light, the provision of professional learning opportunities associated with the National Curriculum might look deprofessionalizing but the fact that complex learning has taken place belies the assumption that the National Curriculum is inherently deprofessionalizing. A closer look at the forms that teachers' continuing learning takes can help to resolve that paradox.

## FORMS OF PROFESSIONAL LEARNING

There has been some scepticism about the general impact of in-service provision in Britain on schools' capacity to change (Bradley *et al.* 1994). And, although professional learning may be associated with attendance at conferences and courses, they are not necessarily the most effective forms of learning (Weimer and Lenze 1991; Bottery and Wright 1996), nor the most significant (Helsby and Knight, 1997). Nevertheless, the introduction of a formal ladder of awards associated with career progression has been prominent in British government thinking about 'new professionalism' in teaching (DfEE 1998).

Table 6.2 summarizes some of the common forms of professional learning. It should be read on the understanding that each of these forms is capable of provoking that reflection that is necessary if fresh understandings are to emerge (Easterby-Smith 1997, p. 1106). Following Day (1993) – and both neo-Piagetian and Vygotskyian thinking – we suggest that this reflection is most powerful when it involves sharing emergent understandings with peers, whose enquiries can support their refinement and consolidation. That anticipates the argument that we shall later propose about the significance of activity systems in teachers' professional development.

The case so far has essentially been that teaching can be seen as a profession partly because the complex learning that was needed to cope with a legion of recent innovations has, in the main, been something that teachers took on and managed themselves, integrating it with the course of their daily work.

The argument that we are about to develop in this section and the next has four strands. (See p. 90.)

**Table 6.2 Some forms of professional learning**

| Form of learning | Possible strengths | Possible problems |
|---|---|---|
| Courses and conferences, off-site | (a) Allow for expertise to be shared with a wide range of teachers<br>(b) Widespread 'default option' – see, for example, reports of professional development in Asia-Pacific Economic Co-operation forum countries (Darling-Hammond and Cobb 1995) | (1) Cost<br>(2) Material may be too general for immediate use in school<br>(3) Ideas need to be translated into school context – this is a skilled and difficult activity<br>(4) Focuses on individual learning detached from the social context in which change is to happen (Smylie 1995) |
| Non-contact days, on-site | (c) Time is available for teachers to work on problems and other matters that concern them<br>(d) Learning takes place with the school (and departmental) context firmly in mind<br>(e) Learning takes place within the social context in which change is to occur | (5) Concern that low-level concerns are addressed: organizing resources, for example<br>(6) Learning may take place through meetings. These may reflect 'contrived' rather than 'true' collegiality (Hargreaves 1994)<br>(7) Lack of outside expertise and perspectives: danger of perpetuating old patterns |
| Staff, departmental and other in-school meetings | See (c)–(e) above | See 5–7 above |
| Subject associations | (f) Source of expert, practitioner-focused advice on curriculum content and on pedagogical content knowledge | (8) Not all teachers are members<br>(9) Some groups' interests (for example primary teachers') can be under-represented<br>(10) Learning is based on print media and tends to be individual, not collegial<br>(11) Problem of translating this into curriculum practice |

**Table 6.2** *continued*

| Reading | (g) A senior official in Ofsted told us that teachers ought to be able to learn what they need by reading books | (12) See 10 & 11 above<br>(13) Suitable books tend to appear after an innovation needs to be in place |
|---|---|---|
| Daily work practices | (h) Learning is a matter of adjusting to and being accommodated within an activity system.<br>(i) Learning is collegial<br>(j) Learning is continuous, not an event<br>(k) Most professional learning is 'informal'<br>(Shapero 1985; Blackler 1993; Becher 1996; Blackler 1995; Eraut 1997) | (14) It's easy for a group, such as a department, to become 'stuck' so that no change takes place, or so that only cosmetic changes take place. In these circumstances, there is no learning<br>(15) People can reinvent the wheel<br>(16) Faulty or inadequate thinking can be perpetuated by norms and routines – no error-checking mechanisms in place |

1. Professional learning is situated, specific and practical in character.
2. Most professional learning takes place in the normal workings of activity systems, such as departments.
3. The main form of professional learning is not through courses and conferences, although they have their place.
4. The improvement of professional learning is contingent upon the improvement of activity systems.

## CONTEXTED LEARNING AND ACTIVITY SYSTEMS

Teachers do not work in isolation, although much of their work is done in separation from their colleagues (Hargreaves 1994). What they do affects what other teachers do and can do. Their expectations, practices and the nature of the learning they foster in children all affect what other teachers do and can do. In this sense, each teacher is a part of a system. As Blackler (1993, p. 875) puts it, 'knowhow is not just a feature of individuals but is distributed within a community'. Systems thinking (Checkland 1981; Checkland and Scholes 1990) claims that a system, such as a community, has 'emergent properties', which are characteristics that are greater than the sum of its parts. These properties can be maximized where people in the system are all working in the same direction. Conversely, where there is little consistency, then systemic attempts to change will be thwarted by the incoherence of the system. So, where teachers are working in similar directions, then system-level effects can be anticipated that will transcend the impact of any of those teachers individually.

But what is a system? According to Checkland, in human affairs a system is what participants see as a system. A fruitful line of research and development involves seeing how different actors define the systems within which they work and then in discussing those different perspectives with them. We describe these groups as 'activity systems' (Blackler 1993), sets of people who are engaged in shared activities. People may belong simultaneously to several different systems – to a course team, to a subject department, and to the whole school. When changes impact upon an activity system, then 'collaborative learning takes place ... [as] communities construct new conceptions of their activities and develop new activity systems' (Blackler 1993, p. 875). Butt and colleagues (1990) argued that much of teachers' professional learning comes about through such 'intercollegiality'.

Care is needed when assuming that any one of these overlapping activity systems is particularly significant in people's working lives. So, it has been widely assumed that the school is a significant organizational unit with emergent properties that make it wise to look for a 'school effect' (for example, Mortimore *et al.* 1988; Smith and Tomlinson 1989). Bradley and colleagues appear to make a similar assumption when writing about professional development (Bradley *et al.* 1994, pp. 233–7). However, recent research seems to be suggesting that the subject department is a more significant unit in secondary schools (Siskin 1994; Talbert and Perry 1994; Harris, Jamieson and Ross 1997; Sammons *et al.* 1997; Gray *et al.* 1999).

Talbert (Talbert and Perry 1994; Talbert 1995) claimed that high-school departments differ quite markedly in the degree to which they support professional learning and in the sorts of professional learning that may (or may not) take place within them. If the department is a prime site for learning, then that learning is contexted and necessarily specific, concerned with reflection about particular practices and possibilities.

The emphasis in this view of learning is that it mainly takes place within the course of work. Consequently it is wrong to act as if it was essentially the product of special events that stand apart from the daily work round. The quality of the work environment, understood as the activity system, is central to this account of professional development. In times of moderate change, the normal course of work often includes curriculum development and action research-like activities of the sort commended by Day (1997). Huberman (1993) has suggested that this development and learning tends to be most effective when it is essentially at the level of 'tinkering' with things. There is some agreement on what characterizes systems that will be more rather than less responsive to greater levels of change. Dubin (1990) suggests that favourable environments are ones in which, amongst other things,

- Job tasks are challenges
- People have responsibility to implement new ideas
- Work is assigned in areas of personal interest
- Free time is available to explore new, advanced ideas
- Recognition and credit are given for good work
- Salary and promotion recommendations are based on performance
- Needs are matched to opportunities to attend courses and technical meetings
- Supervisor encourages independent and innovative thinking
- Supervisor solicits ideas about technical problems
- Performance reviews identify strengths and weaknesses, and directions for improvement
- Innovation is enthusiastically received
- The organization has a progressive atmosphere

- Peers can suggest new approaches based on their experience
- Peers are willing to act as sounding-boards for new ideas.

This interesting set of points is framed for engineering professionals; conflates satisfying and fulfilling factors (Evans 1998); and embodies a rather tidy, rationalistic view of how professional learning may be fostered. Nevertheless, it has value as a framework for thinking about work environments that are effective and conducive to continuous learning.

More recent writings on organizational learning have placed more emphasis on collegial and collaborative cultures as the matrices within which learning takes place. For example, Allee (1997) attaches great importance to 'soft technologies', such as collaborative planning and knowledge-sharing forums which 'facilitate informal exchange, fostering common problem-solving skills and language' (1997, p. 226). Writing about schoolteaching, Hargreaves (1995) noted the potential that collaborative working has for professional development, while also being aware that collaboration can be contrived (1994) and limited by other contextual factors. Similar themes emerge in work on primary schools, with Rosenholtz (1989) saying that 'learning', as opposed to 'stuck', schools were characterized by collegiality and by a belief that children could learn, that teachers could make a difference. (Stuck schools exhibited signs of learned helplessness.)

The position that we have developed, namely that much learning takes place within activity systems, is largely borne out by the responses of informants in the PCT study. Of the 178 teachers involved, 121 returned post-interview questionnaires showing which of thirteen forms of INSET they had participated in the previous twelve months. This gives a picture of their engagement with different forms, although it does not tell us anything about the frequency of that engagement. Their main INSET activities were school-based (43 per cent of the total). Overall, INSET activities were twice as likely to concern subject teaching as to address general and cross-curricular themes.

One hundred and five of these teachers completed a question that asked them what they saw as the best form of professional development. Here, the focus moves from INSET to professional learning in a broader sense. The main response drew attention to the more informal aspects of professional development. Fifty teachers alluded to the value of [informal] working with colleagues, whether in their own school or with teachers from other schools. The flavour of these responses is shown by the endorsements of 'Meeting other teachers, especially within my subject, discussing developments, ideas, etc., cross fertilization of ideas'; 'Conversing with colleagues over current practices and issues, so sense and degree of isolation is reduced'; and 'Being given the time and opportunity to talk to other teachers – learn their strategies for dealing with situations'.

A pre-interview questionnaire asked about influences on their professional development. The most frequent response, coming from 86 of the 147 returning this questionnaire, was that teachers' own experience was an important influence, closely followed by colleagues in the same department (77 cases) and their own beliefs and convictions (74 cases). When asked which was the most important influence upon their professional development, the 124 who replied put experience at the head of the list (40 cases), followed by colleagues in the same department and by their own beliefs (23 cases each). Initial teacher education (ITE) was ranked fourth, both in terms of frequency and of importance, while formal INSET activities were eighth in terms of frequency. Only four of the 124 respondents said that INSET was the most important form of professional development for them.

These data point to the importance of school-centred INSET and, more importantly, to the primacy in professional development of activities that lay outside formal, mandated provision, whether in or out of school. Our stance is that learning takes place within activity systems such as departments. In times of mandated change, especially when time is tight, access to outside provision is restricted and situation-specific learning is necessary to accomplish situation-specific changes, then far and away the most important learning takes place in activity systems. Plainly, there are disadvantages if contact with other departments and other ideas is restricted, since insularity, low expectations and error may all ensue. For that reason, if for no other, access to formal provision remains an important complement to 'the learning department'.

What are the implications of this theoretical analysis for thinking about 'new professionalism'?

## BETTER PROFESSIONAL LEARNING

As we have said, government concern to enhance the standing of teaching in England – the promotion of 'new professionalism' – has centred upon the development of a ladder of professional development awards and close scrutiny of the quality of INSET provision. Associated with these moves are a renewed interest in the appraisal system and higher pay for high-performing teachers. These innovations should enhance teachers' continued development, although there is room for argument about the extent to which they support *professional* development and about the exact nature of 'new professionalism' itself. Ladders, courses, awards and incentives are familiar and thoroughly traditional responses to the need for better professional development. When located within a framework of lifelong learning, they can be flexible and more effective as responses. The catch is that close attention to better systems of formal professional development can distract attention from the more important task of creating workplaces that are rich learning environments. Although we have not talked of 'the learning organization', since it is too ambitious and too grand a concept, we have been saying something similar, namely that the quality of the workplace as a learning environment is crucial to professional development. Attempts to foster a 'new professionalism' that do not tackle the school and the department as sites of learning will be limited.

We have argued that the emotional aspects of professional learning ought not to be neglected, but the position we have developed implies that the main way of attending to them is through looking at the emotional climate of the department. There is here a fortunate convergence between the ideas about learned optimism and thinking about what makes for a learning department. In both cases there is an insistence on things such as collegiality; trust; a concern for people; a belief that people naturally try to do well; listening to one another; a tolerance of mistakes made in good faith; a commitment to learning, growth and improvement; and the pursuit of shared values in individual ways. Although such thinking is to be found in many international works on management in general (for example, Hesselbein *et al.* 1996), it may be criticized on two grounds. First, it exaggerates the degree to which cultures may be created or reshaped (Myerson and Martin 1997). Second, collegiality is left as an ill-defined concept (Little 1992), for which rather exaggerated, somewhat naive, claims can be made (Bush 1997; Easterby-Smith 1997). Sometimes, especially when a system is under pressure to make rapid changes, a more directed and less collegial approach is needed. Yet, notwithstanding these reservations, we suggest that here is a direction that is worthy of pursuit on three grounds. One is that it is a direction that is regularly endorsed in the wider literature on management and organizational learning. A second is that it is the only model of learning in activity systems – the alternative is to conceptualize professional learning as something that mainly takes place outside the daily work environment, which is a position we have rejected. The third is that it is a model which squares with our values and with those expressed in the rhetoric of the teachers with whom we spoke – it is a professional model of learning.

However, some of our informants told us that managerialism was more evident in their schools. They talked of a more visible and active management team that was more directive and, in some cases, called teachers more vigorously to account. It is useful at this point to draw briefly on the work of Douglas McGregor (McGregor 1960). McGregor divides managers into two main categories: 'Theory X' managers who tend to assume that employees do not want to work, are not interested in improving their performance and therefore need close supervision, while 'Theory Y' managers tend to assume the opposite. The evidence from our informants suggests that there has been a return to 'Theory X' views of management, with an emphasis on control and the exercise of power over subordinates. Quite apart from such developments, whose incidence is not known, there are bound to be heads of department who routinely manage on Theory X principles, not on the Theory Y principles that we have endorsed. If Theory Y is compatible with the approach to professional learning that we have outlined here and Theory X is not, then there is an important implication for the preparation of departmental leaders. More generally, there is a need to consider preparation for departmental leadership rather than just preparation for departmental management, always assuming that current management preparation is itself adequate.

Strikingly, we heard almost nothing about training for departmental management (or administration) and nothing about the broader concept of departmental leadership. The following quotation clarifies the difference:

> This book argues that management, although important, is not enough to make an organization successful ... [Leadership] is that package of personal qualities that focuses on the emotional side of directing organizations. Its dimensions are symbolic, charismatic, inspirational, and highly personal ... [Leaders] shape the organization's ethical climate and culture .... (Barach and Eckhardt 1996, p. 4)

Although there is an extensive and popular literature on leadership in general, in education the concept is virtually unknown. It is true that Harris, Jamieson and Ross (1997) have described features of effective secondary school departments that appear to be conducive to continued professional learning. However, their study was not designed to explore professional learning and it could be said that their list of indicators of effectiveness is over-determined – there are quite simply too many of them. Consequently, they are able to say little about leadership for professional learning, especially as they found two principal models of leadership: one that dwelt upon the operation of good structures and another that concentrated on the formation of culture.

We have drawn on evidence about teachers' professional development with the onset of the National Curriculum and upon a range of theories to develop a distinctive view of professional development. We suggest that a priority for any vision of a new professionalism is to promote leadership that will help all subject departments to move as far as possible to becoming sites of continuous professional learning, complementing the TTA's developments of formal INSET opportunities. On this view, the future of professional learning is bound up with the quality of professional learning about departmental leadership.

Teachers' professional development is a politically contested matter. While it is hardly a party political issue, it is one that involves a range of interests. On one side there is an implicit view of teachers (and other workers in the welfare provision sector) as directed technicians who need to acquire routine knowledge and skills to be deployed. Others are sceptical about beliefs that evidence-based medicine, let alone evidence-based teaching, can yield prescriptions that override the need for judgement. Furthermore, they argue that professionals should have a responsibility to consider clients' best interests, which involves reflecting on and choosing goals in the interests of public and individual good: Woods *et al.* (1998) address this in the context of educational markets and Bottery (1998) with respect to teacher professionalism.

Associated with that are political differences about the sites of teachers' professional development, which merge into disputes about who controls it. Concentration upon formal provision can be seen as an extension of the technicist agenda, while promotion of the 'learning department' inclines power to the teachers and implies a different notion of professionalism from that of those whose thinking assumes top-down, centre–periphery control of teachers' work. Moreover, the features that we have identified with 'learning departments' are broadly similar to characteristics that are effective at fostering students' learning (Harris, Jamieson and Ross 1997; Sammons *et al.* 1997; Gray *et al.* 1999).

One political point can hardly be contested. If teachers are the key to continually raising standards, then their professional development becomes an urgent investment priority. Better professional development can enhance teachers' skills and under-standings in ways that are closely connected to the work setting. Where professional development is understood as a necessity for organizational learning and for the growth of effective ways of working, and where it is seen to contribute to teachers' ability to find fulfilment in their work, then it is easy to argue that it can be seen as a sensitive indicator of what an occupation is really about. What is clear is that attempts to enhance teachers' skills have so far been neither well-conceptualized, nor well-funded.

*Chapter 7*

# The Professional Nature of Teachers' Work

With the erosion in the 1980s of the tradition or myth that teaching should be taken as a profession because teachers had considerable control of the curriculum came two stances. One was that teaching was being deprofessionalized, while the other held that nothing of importance had been lost. This has been seen in broad terms in Part 1 and in detail in the discussion of teachers and the curriculum in Chapter 5. The exploration of the provision for continuous learning for teachers indicated that new demands made upon them could be interpreted as indicators that teaching was even being reprofessionalized. Certainly, at the turn of the century, commentators in several countries are proposing that there is a need for a 'new professionalism'. At that point it is appropriate to return to the PCT data, to locate it alongside evidence about other changes in teachers' workplaces and open up the idea that old, broad-brush arguments over the professionalism of teaching are redundant in the face of more nuanced, complex and contexted analyses.

## DIMENSIONS OF PROFESSIONAL WORK: TEACHERS' PERSPECTIVES

In this section we summarize responses to four prompts used in the first round of PCT interviews, which involved 178 teachers. The Appendix contains a fuller account of the research design.

The following prompts were used to investigate teachers' thinking about the professional nature of their work.

3. Asked about the extent to which informants saw teaching as a profession [respondents had previously talked about professions *in general* and what identified an occupation as a profession].
7. Asked how they would identify one teacher as more professional than another.
4. Asked what, if anything, there was in their work *as a subject teacher* that could be identified as 'professional'.
8. Explored whether there had been changes in the degree to which teaching could be regarded as a profession.

**Table 7.1 Summary of responses to four prompts about the professional nature of teachers' work**

| Features of professional work in teaching | Prompt 3 | Prompt 7 | Prompt 4 | Prompt 8 |
|---|---|---|---|---|
| Appearance | 7 | | | |
| Autonomy | 6 | | | −2 |
| Conscientiousness | 2 | 1 | 2 | −1 |
| Interpersonal | 5 | 2 | | |
| Knowledge | 1 | 4 | 1 | |
| Organization | | | 3 | |
| Personal qualities | | 5 | | |
| Pupil behaviour | | 3 | | −3 |
| Standing | 3 | | | −4 |
| Values judgements | 4 | | | |

Notes: Glossary of terms used in Column 1, with illustrative quotations

| | |
|---|---|
| Appearance | 'Suit and short haircut' |
| Autonomy | Professionals exercise autonomy in non-routine decision-making |
| Conscientiousness | All references to planning, diligence, commitment, etc. |
| Interpersonal | Professionals work well with others – colleagues, parents, pupils |
| Knowledge | Professionals have specialist knowledge, through qualification, experience or both |
| Organization | A professional teacher is a good organizer and manager in the classroom |
| Personal qualities | Professionals have certain personal qualities, apart from conscientiousness |
| Pupil behaviour | Pupils behave well when taught by a professional teacher |
| Standing | Respect, status, including the way these are reflected in pay |
| Values judgements | Professionals make judgements reflecting their values |

Table 7.1 summarizes the main categories of response to these four prompts that bear on different aspects of the same concept, professionalism. The numbers in Columns 2–5 indicate rank order. Some questions generated more responses and more complex responses, so there is not the same number of ranks in each column. Responses to Prompt 8 indicated that teachers thought that this feature was threatened or had been harmed by changes to the educational system. For that reason, all ranks in Column 5 are shown as negative numbers. So, the ability to do the job well – conscientiousness in the table – was seen to be the most significant casualty of recent changes to education.

In addition to the comments about the professional nature of teachers' work that are summarized in the table, there were abundant references to intensification, in the form of frequent changes in government requirements, new expectations, the increase in record-keeping and accountability activities, the impact of Ofsted inspections, the proliferation of meetings, and such like.

In the sociological literature there are two main approaches to classifying occupations as professions. One is to compare the occupation with a list of traits, which are typically descriptive of an idealized view of law and medicine in Anglo-Saxon societies. The other focuses upon the standing of an occupation, arguing that a profession is what people say is a profession. Teachers' reasoning about their work was dominated by the trait approach. Teaching, they said, was a profession if it exhibited certain characteristics, although there were some replies that suggested that the standing of the occupation was crucial to claims that teaching is a profession. Questions about changes in teachers' work produced claims that teaching's occupational standing had diminished (Prompt 8).

A notable characteristic of the set of features is how few of them are distinctive of a profession. They may all be necessary in an occupation that aspires to be called a profession, but conscientiousness would be expected in any job and interpersonal skills in most. Furthermore while it takes skill to be well-organized and a good manager in the classroom, to have pupils behave well, those might be seen as occupational skills, rather than defining characteristics of a profession. A number of features on this list might be described as traits that are necessary but not sufficient for an occupation to be designated a profession within trait theory. However, in that theory, knowledge, autonomy and the making of non-routine decisions would rate very highly. Their ranking by teachers is therefore of interest.

Different prompts elicited very different patterns of response. That reminds us of a fact that is well known in psychology, namely that small variations in questions can produce sharp variations in response. However, we want to go beyond that methodological point by suggesting that the idea of a profession is a heavily contexted one. The concepts that were volunteered in response to Prompt 3, which asked, in general terms, about teaching as a profession, differed from those in response to Prompt 7. In the same vein, responses to the prompt about the professional nature of subject teaching (Prompt 4) was less wide-ranging than thinking elicited by prompts 3 and 7. That is not to say that subject teaching does not involve traits elicited by those two prompts. It is more likely that the request to think about the professional nature of subject teaching accessed a somewhat different script – that of knowledge in use rather than espoused knowledge (Schön 1983) – and produced answers that complemented, not contradicted, responses to the other two prompts. That calls into question analyses of teacher professionality and deprofessionalization that treat the idea of teaching as a profession as a simple, one-dimensional matter. The pattern of responses in Table 7.1 indicates that teachers' perception of the degree to which their work is professional, and of the extent to which professional standing is under threat, vary according to context.

Furthermore, although this is not shown in Table 7.1, there are considerable variations in the sample of 178 respondents. Individually, each differed from another, reflecting their life histories, school and departmental settings, subject allegiances, and so on. Teaching is a highly contexted activity and teachers' analyses were as individual as the contexts within which they worked. Table 7.1 is an act of generalization that does some violence to the individuality of the respondents. There is another sense in which Table 7.1 oversimplifies matters. The sample was constructed to give a balance of respondents from each of three subject areas – maths, technology and humanities – and in each subject there was an almost perfect balance of men and women. Given research suggesting that the work experience of men and women teachers differs, and given research into the ways in which different subjects impact upon secondary school teachers' lives, it could be expected that there would be some differences between teachers according to gender and subject. It would also be predicted that the common experience of teaching would make for similarities as well. Since the core concern of this project was to talk with teachers to help them to construct an account of the extent to which their work felt professional, it would be quite inappropriate to test for differences between the sub-groups with statistical techniques. That is doubly so, given what we have said about the analysis of the data. However, although formal testing was not in order, it is possible to see some substantial differences between subgroups, always in the recognition that differences are not consistent across prompts: the pattern of situated accounts of the professional nature of the job is perpetuated in analysis at the sub-group level. The next two paragraphs report these substantial differences.

Men made more references to Autonomy (Prompt 3 – and to its erosion, Prompt 8) and to Knowledge (Prompt 4 and to a lesser extent, Prompt 3). Women made more references to the standing of the occupation (Prompt 3 – and to its erosion in response to Prompt 8).

Examining the data by subject groups yielded the following striking differences. Humanities teachers made more references to Autonomy (Prompt 3 – and to its erosion, Prompt 8); to Conscientiousness (Prompts 7 and 4); and to pupil behaviour (in Prompt 8 identifying a decline in it). Maths teachers made more references to Knowledge (Prompts 7 and 4) and to Interpersonal skills (Prompt 3). They made the fewest references to the standing of the occupation (Prompt 3) and to pupil behaviour (Prompt 7 – and to its erosion, Prompt 8). Technology teachers made the most references to Conscientiousness in response to Prompt 3 and the fewest in response to Prompt 4. They made the fewest references to a loss of Autonomy (Prompt 8).

Our preferred reading of these data is that they show three things. First, we must not lose sight of the variations within any sub-set of teachers, showing the degree to which structural changes in education are mediated by the contingencies of specific sites (schools and departments, for example) and again by teachers' individual situations and identities. Our data are consistent with the position adopted by Halford and Leonard (1999):

> Employees in the public sector come to work with their own personal agenda, such that the degree to which their reality is changed by new discourses in the workplace is highly variable. Certainly restructuring might mean the presentation of alternative discourses offering new possibilities for self-hood. However, we cannot assume that this is in any way an automatic or linear process, or that individuals respond in ways which are consistent or coherent. (p.120)

Second, there are some noticeable variations by sub-group in their patterns of thinking about the professional nature of their work. Third, the variations must be seen against a background of similarity of thinking. The picture, then, is of individual and sub-cultural variations nested within a broader culture of teaching that is formed partly by similar patterns of socialization and by the shared experience of working in similar organizations, doing similar tasks under similar conditions.

We note that it would be possible, on the basis of these data, to compile profiles of each sub-group in terms of its thinking about the professional nature of teaching. We have resisted doing so, partly because of the underlying similarities and partly because it is not clear what the value would be of doing so.

In short, we have used data from interviews with 178 secondary school teachers to claim that:

- Their thinking about the professional nature of their work is contexted and complex – 'identities cannot merely be "read off" from a given context, but may take many forms, and may encompass individual practices of modification and resistance' (Halford and Leonard 1999, p. 103);
- Their thinking conforms closely with the trait theory of professions;

- Their thinking is contexted: facets emphasized in one context are less evident in another;
- There are considerable similarities amongst teachers, regardless of gender or teaching subject: there are also notable variations;
- When analysing the professional aspects of their work, teachers were sensitive to the whole complex of government interventions, although they gave prominence to National Curriculum changes.

Having examined how the professional issue looked from the teachers' point of view, we look at it from two other angles. The first is from the point of view of people of national significance in the educational community, where data from interviews with key informants will be the source. The second moves from a fascination with curriculum to a broader focus on educational change.

## KEY INFORMANTS' PERSPECTIVES

We interviewed thirteen people who had been prominent in the post-1988 educational changes, whether as politicians, inspectors, local authority officers, policy-makers, or because they were involved with teacher education or with National Curriculum development and policy. Plainly, a sample of thirteen does not adequately represent the policy community, whatever that might be, but their opinions do give an indication of the way teaching's professional standing was seen by those whose concerns had to go beyond the more situated ones of the teachers we interviewed.

The question of the professional standing of teachers was not seen as particularly a British concern: 'it's also under debate in other countries – France too, the States, Australia, all seem to be on about this' (former senior HMI); nor as one peculiar to teaching: 'I would say that practically any profession you approached ... they'll say status has been eroded' (prominent national policy adviser). One informant added: 'talking to friends in other professions, they're also pretty disillusioned with their professions ... I think it's a late-twentieth-century phenomenon' (chief education officer). Nor were teachers the only ones who could manipulate the claim to be a profession: 'Certainly, it's not ... only teachers who on occasion hide behind their professionalism or false professionalism. Doctors do it, lawyers do it, policemen do it, it's not only teachers' (senior member of Ofsted).

All of the informants felt that teaching had the potential to be a profession – 'I don't think teaching does look like it at the moment, that's my position. I think it ought to, however, and I think a lot of its remedies lie in its own hands' (former senior civil servant and vice-chancellor). Most of these informants thought that teaching *was*, at that point, a profession, although there was the comment that, 'I think it ["professional"] may be a word which is almost past its sell-by date in the twenty-first century' (former politician and vice-chancellor). Accounts of what made teaching a profession differed. On the one hand:

> I think a reflective teacher is most certainly something that is a very important part, but by no means the only part, of being a professional teacher ... reflective in the sense that they place the activity within the broader context, because education is placed within a broader context, cultural context, context of social policy, and so on ... but there's more to it than that ... a code of conduct, a sense of propriety and a set of values.    (senior SCAA official)

On the other:

> the ideal of the teacher as a reflective practitioner doesn't seem to have done much good. Let's have teachers who can teach effectively and they will become more professional as they become more effective and they will become more valued as a profession. Proof of the pudding is in the learning of the children. Hardly in the reflectiveness of the practitioner ... The essence of professionalism for me is ethical. It depends on one's stance to what one does, rather than the skills that the day-to-day delivery of the service that one gives.
>
> (senior Ofsted officer)

There was consensus that the problems of teaching's professional standing pre-dated the reforms of the late 1980s:

> If that [1985] was the point at which professionalism finally died, we haven't moved very far from that since. We're bumping along the bottom ... In the medium term teaching simply has to become more of a profession. Things simply cannot get worse.
>
> (senior TTA official)

> [In the mid 1980s] ... a distinct degree of non-professional behaviour had gone on.
>
> (former senior HMI)

> I'm convinced that they are becoming and have become more professional, I've no doubt about that.
>
> (senior SCAA official)

There was, then, an emphatic rejection of the claim that the National Curriculum had deskilled teachers – many of these informants argued it reskilled them:

> *Interviewer:* ... there is a view that teachers are being changed from being professionals to being technicians, to being deskilled. Do you have a view on that?
> *Informant:* I do. I don't agree ... Some teachers have gone into 'nose dive' mode about their worth and their value to society. They sometimes see themselves as deskilled. I don't agree with that. But because they are not in a profession – they are not organized properly – ... they have no way of combating what comes at them from the media ... and politicians.
>
> (senior TTA official)

> In the case of the secondary curriculum, it ought to be fairly clear that the freedom was never that great if you took GCSE and its predecessors seriously ... in a way it [the National Curriculum] has certainly reduced the capacity of teachers to influence or determine the curriculum, but one has to remember that it was a capacity that often was not exercised.
>
> (former senior DES official)

> [Teachers in France] are proud to have the standards, they don't mind the fact that on a Monday morning or whatever it is everybody is doing mathematics or whatever it is in a particular way and so on *et cetera, et cetera*. I think that's been again another alibi that's been used and a misunderstanding, actually, of what at heart a profession is about. And a profession is not about a licence to do anything you want in any way you want, treating the customer in any way that you can.
>
> (former civil servant and vice-chancellor)

> The National Curriculum, if it's done nothing else, it's made teachers far more articulate about what the curriculum is, what it's for and their part in it, and that was bound to have an effect on professionalism ... I think the erosion of teacher professionalism took place in the Seventies and Eighties, insofar as there were any things to erode, and it hasn't had anything to do with any of these things that have happened since.
>
> (former senior curriculum adviser)

Likewise, there was consensus that teachers' claim to professional expertise rested on pedagogy, not on curriculum-making:

> I don't think that curricular freedom is at the heart of teachers' professionalism. At the heart of their profession is pedagogy ... at the core of teachers' responsibility has always been delivery, not the content of what is delivered.
>
> (senior TTA official)

> What I do feel strongly is that curriculum is far too serious a matter to be left to be decided by teachers.                                                        (former senior DES official)

Not only did the 1988 Education Act 'put in law for the first time that matters of methodology, materials, teaching materials, subject matter and so on are for teachers to determine' (former senior HMI), but informants felt that there were plenty of 'spaces' to be found in the new system:

> The scope for them to determine what they do in their schools and in their classrooms, I don't think it's reduced as much as many of them perceive it to be, but it is reduced and the way many of them are reacting, understandably, is reducing it even more ... in that more teachers are now ready ... to be told what to do because of all the damn changes that have happened.                                                        (former senior HMI)

> *Interviewer:* Has teachers' capacity to make decisions about the curriculum changed?
> *Informant:* Oh yes. Not capacity. Teachers' courage has changed, teachers' courage has been weakened over the last ten years ... I think it's all to do with courage, it's all to do with personal courage to say 'Sod it' to authority: 'I'll do it my way' – Frank Sinatra.
>                                                        (former politician and vice-chancellor)

In other words, teachers could be blamed for not having seen that the National Curriculum set bounds within which they had 'greater freedom, discrimination and choice' (former senior curriculum adviser). Indeed, there was a view that teachers had created some of the pressures that they claimed were crushing them. For example:

> I think there's a vast amount of unnecessary ... 'professional' in inverted commas, activity going on which is quite often a distraction from the real work of the school. But more of it is self-imposed than imposed from without ... [for example, schemes of work] instead of being the half a side of A4, which is what they probably ought to be, I mean they run to pages and pages. And they're full of dreadful curriculum and assessment speak ... a lot of things that go into preparing for inspections aren't necessary but schools in a climate of anxiety do these things.                                                        (senior SCAA official)

Other informants did not go so far, recognizing that, as some of our teacher informants had said, Ofsted inspections exerted their own, very real force on the curriculum:

> It's not the weak teacher who goes off sick as soon as Ofsted is mentioned [that is the problem], it's the damage that is being done to motivated teachers, to good teachers who feel threatened by a process that they feel doesn't, in some cases, begin to address the very real problems that they, as teachers in that school, with that class, have to address on a day-to-day basis.                                                        (Conservative politician and educationist)

> ... a legislated curriculum ... tends to become too rigid [and] ... I think we have accentuated that by the ... external forms of assessment and league tables and by the way the Ofsted inspection is ...                                                        (former senior HMI)

Yet, whatever worries there were about the possible 'curriculum backwash' of Ofsted inspections and SATs, there was unanimity that teaching, to be seen as a profession, had to be accountable – '[Teachers] have not yet properly come to terms with ... quite – certainly – sensible and really quite elementary notions of accountability' (former senior DES official). There were disagreements about the form that accountability should take. One the one hand,

> It seems to me that by dint of your education and training [being] at such a level, people should say 'well we are assuring quality by appointing people who have done that. Now it's up to them, they are the people who should take decisions and react' ... Whereas ... we are not in that position, we don't actually trust the teachers at the moment ... we've got to get to that state [trusting the teachers]. If we don't, then it's going to be pretty disastrous – I mean we won't raise standards.                                                        (former senior HMI)

On the other hand, most informants preferred an inspection-based system, although the chief education officer inclined towards an LEA-based system that would be committed to continuous quality improvement through the promotion and dissemination of evidence-based teaching.

From the perspectives of these informants, teaching was improving its image, and its professional standing was growing or poised to grow, if teachers would

- Be seen to be concerned about improving standards, rather than risk caricature as an occupation devoted to self-interested trade-unionism;
- Exploit the opportunities offered by the National Curriculum – find and exploit the spaces;
- Avoid becoming prisoners of what they took to be the National Curriculum requirements;
- Develop better links with parents and the community at large, even though 'an awful lot of teachers are actually rather bad with adults' (former senior DES official);
- Dress properly (former senior curriculum adviser).

Or, as a chief education officer put it:

> it does seem to me now that teachers really have to start to get hold of the curriculum and to shout about what they succeed at – and they do succeed a lot – and in a sense re-establish a sense of pride in the profession ... in a sense, teaching has been reduced to a kind of ... technician's approach to life and I think education's the worse for that.

The striking thing was that even informants who appear to be hostile to teachers had both insight and concern for their position. What may not be so welcome is that, just as our teacher informants blamed central agencies for their plight, our key informants, while recognizing some defects and rigidities in the early versions of the National Curriculum, argued that teachers had themselves largely created that of which they complained. Where teachers' accounts of the professional nature of their work centred on the vicissitudes of daily life, the key informants saw matters in terms of teachers regaining a trust that had been lost in the mid-1980s, of accountability, and of raising standards. As others have suggested (Evans 1998; Bottery 1998), teachers were concerned with practical daily issues arising from educational changes, not with the issues that have occupied academics and policy commentators. For example, they explained that they were professionals because they had gained knowledge through initial training and experience. Unlike commentators on professions, they did not refer to the complexity of that knowledge, nor to the skilled judgements that lay behind its use, with the result that their claims looked similar to the claims of other workers, who also have to possess knowledge. This mismatch of perspectives has bedevilled the development of the National Curriculum. Teachers assert the primacy of nuts-and-bolts classroom practices and have reservations about government actions that are proclaimed as attempts to raise standards:

> The people who write the Orders aren't in the classroom. They're probably highly qualified and intellectual but they're out of touch with reality.          (history teacher)

And in the eyes of key informants, it almost seems that concentrating on the difficulties of classroom practice is an impediment to the development of teaching as a profession, which involves addressing system-wide policy issues. Two recent research studies have argued that policy issues must be addressed if standards are to be improved (Bottery 1998; Woods *et al.* 1998) and if teaching is to stand as a profession (Bottery 1998). But at the moment, practitioners and policy-shapers appear to be separated by different discourses: a discourse of problems on the one hand, of possibilities on the other. There may be a reconciliation of the two perspectives in the recent suggestion that schools that continue to improve strongly are schools that consistently attend to the improvement of classroom teaching (Gray *et al.* 1999). The suggestion in Chapter 6 that the department is the natural site for continuing professional learning points in the same direction.

At this point it is appropriate to gaze beyond conclusions that are largely related to the implementation of the National Curriculum and consider the cumulative impact of other systemic changes that were impacting upon secondary schools in the 1990s.

## PROFESSIONALISM AND MULTIPLE STRUCTURAL CHANGES

As indicated at the beginning of Part 2, teacher professionalism in the 1990s is affected not only by changes brought about by the introduction of the National Curriculum, but also by

> a massive interconnected policy ensemble, a complex of projects, initiatives, schemes, agencies, imperatives and legislation, which is pushing education in new directions and affecting the way teachers work, the way schools are run and organised and the nature and delivery of the school curriculum.                                    (Ball 1990, p. 98)

In England, as in many other Westernized nations, the public education system has become an important political priority, and there has been an unprecedented accumulation of top-down directives, ministerial interventions and legislative initiatives that have profoundly changed the structures and frameworks that shape teachers' work and within which the notion of teacher professionalism is contested on a day-to-day basis. Overall, there has been a conspicuous tightening of these frameworks by central government (Helsby 1999) and an ostensible diminution of choice within schools as 'teaching has become more tension-ridden and constrained' (Woods *et al.* 1997). A whole series of public discourses and policy initiatives has sought to reconstruct the notion of a 'good teacher' and appears to have redefined the teacher's role away from that of an autonomous member of a professional group and towards that of a skilled and compliant employee:

> the version of the teacher that is being redesigned is individualistic rather than collective in orientation, differentiated not homogeneous, competent not responsible. From the employer's point of view, professionalism would be seen as an individual attribute, something the teacher has or will acquire.                                    (Lawn 1996, p. 119)

Recent education policies have consistently encouraged growing differentiation and increased competition between schools, between departments and between individual teachers. The deliberate and overt promotion of 'choice and diversity' (DFE/WO 1992) has had a profound effect not only upon the organization and management of education but also upon the prevailing value orientation where '*technocratic managerialism*' is asserted 'over and above what might be termed *ethical professionalism*' (Ball 1994, p. 138). Of particular significance in this respect has been the displacement in policy-making circles of Keynesian ideals of public service by the tenets of the 'new public management' (Hood 1991; Bottery 1996). This influential discourse tends to reject the notion of public sector workers as dedicated professionals, applying their specialist knowledge to further the well-being of their clients. Instead, it depicts them as self-interested individuals, motivated by extrinsic rewards and in need of management and regulation.

One of the most obvious of the Conservative government's structural changes in the organization of the education service has been the steady dismantling of LEA bureaucracies and the devolution of budgets and of management responsibilities to individual institutions. The enforced introduction through the 1988 Education Reform Act of a system of local management of schools (LMS) and the further provision for schools to 'opt out' of local education authority control entirely by becoming grant-maintained schools (GMS) significantly weakened the LEAs and curtailed their local support services (Levacic 1995). Their vulnerability was further increased by subsequent measures, including the withdrawal of much of the central funding for LEA inspection and advisory services, the removal of further education, tertiary and sixth-form colleges from LEA control, and the creation of independent City Technology Colleges in direct competition with LEA comprehensive schools (Simon and Chitty 1993). The effects of these changes were not only a reduction in locally organized services for teachers, including INSET courses, advisory support and teachers' centres, but also a move away from local planning and towards more decision-making at institutional level. As former Chief HMI Eric Bolton points out, it is

> a triumph of hope over experience to expect that such self-interested, isolated, fragmented decisions, made in thousands of separate institutions, will add up to a sensible, effective and efficient national school system.                          (Bolton 1993, p. 8)

This fragmentation was further encouraged by Conservative government attempts to increase competition between schools through exposure to market forces. As well as devolving resource management to schools, the 1988 ERA also introduced a new system of parental choice and pupil-related funding, whereby resource allocations were determined by the numbers of pupils which a school was able to recruit. In a climate of severe financial constraints, this put pressure upon institutions to compete with each other, rather than working together and sharing good practice, as they often had in the past. This was certainly the view of one headteacher, interviewed in 1997:

> Collaboration between schools is now minimal ... it's part of the new agenda: if we do something interesting, there's a strategy of playing the cards close to your chest in the new competitive climate. The national agenda of competition has put the skids under the sharing of good practice.

Thus, many teachers tended to become more isolated within their institutions, as the diminution or loss of advisory support was matched by a lessening of contacts with teachers from other schools.

Within the school itself, LMS had further implications for teachers' work, as headteachers and other senior managers took on new responsibilities for managing both the budget and the workforce and for negotiating with their recently empowered school governors (Evetts 1994a). Not only were these responsibilities very time-consuming, reducing the time available for day-to-day involvement in curriculum matters and regular face-to-face contact with classroom teachers, but there were also pressures from Ofsted and from the officially sponsored management training schemes to develop technical-rational approaches to school management. According to many commentators, these factors combined to influence the work culture of headship away from educational and moral leadership and towards professional business management (Evetts 1994b; McHugh and McMullen 1995; Gewirtz *et al.* 1995; Webb and Vulliamy 1996; Power *et al.* 1997). At the same time, the new organizational arrangements tended to reaffirm the 'managerial prerogative' (Menter *et al.* 1997) and to redistribute institutional authority away from teachers and towards teacher managers. The latter had greater access to in-service courses through which they gained knowledge and understanding of, and developed skills in, the new management techniques. The underlying economic rationalism of these approaches fostered sets of values in schools that were often at variance with the deeply held principles of many teachers. Thus the new business emphasis upon competition, economy, efficiency and effectiveness often came into conflict with traditional professional and ethical values such as collaboration, equity and social justice.

Whilst headteachers varied in the extent to which they supported and promoted these imperatives, classroom teachers had less opportunity to impose their beliefs. Not only were the power differentials in school changed in favour of senior managers, but organizational transformations tended to create or reinforce divisions between teachers in different departments and to make it more difficult for them to take concerted action. In some cases, reduced opportunities for job mobility and career advancement allowed headteachers to encourage a more competitive atmosphere between staff. More widely, the subject-specific basis of the National Curriculum and internal competition between departments for resources were said to be divisive and to reinforce the 'balkanisation' of school cultures (Hargreaves 1992; Reay 1998). At the same time, increased workloads (Campbell and Neill 1994a; 1994b) were inhibiting sociability and reducing the opportunities for collegial working, despite a clear increase in in-school meetings (Helsby 1999).

Thus, increasing isolation of teachers from external sources of support was matched by an ostensible decline in empowering forms of collaboration between teachers in schools, and some growth in distance between teachers and the school's senior managers. The time-honoured principle of 'divide and rule' may be relevant here, since isolated individuals are far easier to manipulate and control than a cohesive and unified workforce. However, such simplistic and mechanistic views of human behaviour do not generally reflect the complexities of real life, since individuals may always resist and contest the intentions of educational reformers. Indeed Wallace (1998) develops the notion of a 'counter-policy', whereby schools and colleges may, for example, subvert the intended marketization of education by deliberately continuing to collaborate, despite the competitive climate. The same holds true for departments and for individuals.

The extent to which individual teachers or groups of teachers actively contest or subvert external imperatives is variable. A key factor in determining their response is the level of their *professional confidence*:

> Professional confidence implies a belief both in one's authority and in one's capacity to make important decisions about the conduct of one's work [and] the feeling of coping with the work in hand and being 'in control': this implies that the individual is not confronted with excessive and overwhelming work demands which necessitate constant 'corner-

cutting' and ill-considered activity, but rather that there is some scope to reflect upon, and
decide between, alternative approaches or courses of action.     (Helsby 1995, pp. 324–5)

Where confidence is high, teachers are likely to regard policies merely as suggested
courses of action and to seek to impose their own professional interpretations upon
them (something commended by a number of our key informants.) Where confidence
is low, however, they are more amenable to external direction and manipulation.

There is considerable evidence to suggest that the professional confidence of many
teachers was adversely affected by the educational reforms, especially in the early
stages. First, their role as key decision-makers was repeatedly undermined by the
profession's virtual exclusion from the consultative processes preceding major reforms,
by the increased demands for greater public accountability and surveillance and also by
the constant 'discourses of derision' (Ball 1990) voiced by politicians and other public
figures, including the repeated references by Her Majesty's Chief Inspector of Schools
to 'failing teachers' and 'failing schools'. Second, the fact that the reforms required
teachers to develop new knowledge and skills and to change their practices in line with
an externally constructed agenda was suggestive of a process of deskilling (Ozga 1995),
whilst the extent and pace of continued change diminished the confidence and sapped
the resilience of many experienced teachers. Third, reduced resources and the general
intensification of working life (Apple 1986; Hargreaves 1994) often made it difficult for
teachers to feel 'in control' or to engage in reflective practice as opposed to crisis
management. As a result, many experienced a loss of autonomy along with increased
activity and stress (Gewirtz 1997). Fourth, legally enforced changes in teachers' terms
and conditions of service, including a contractual specification of minimum working
hours and an explicit and extended itemization of duties, were viewed as an affront to
the deep professional commitment of the majority of teachers and could be seen as part
of a general process of deprofessionalization. Indeed Ball (1994, p. 49) has identified
'an increase in technical elements of teachers' work and a reduction in the professional', with the result that the 'spaces for professional autonomy and judgement are
[further] reduced'.

Given these extensive changes, it is hardly surprising that so many teachers' self-
image suffered as they experienced a loss of professional confidence. In extreme cases,
this resulted in stress and burn-out (Woods and Jeffrey 1997), in others it led to
diminished responsibility and reluctant compliance, as teachers took the easy way out
and did the minimum necessary to meet the requirements. However, there was also
some evidence of teachers engaging in 'creative mediation' (Osborn 1997), gaining new
professional skills (Campbell and Neill 1994a) and becoming reprofessionalized as well
as deprofessionalized (Hargreaves and Goodson 1996). Thus, whilst the tightened
frameworks within which teachers were now working may, at first sight, have made it
more difficult for them to regard themselves, and to act, as 'professionals', it was by no
means impossible. As Fullan (1991, p. 49) reminds us, '[c]hanging formal structures is
not the same as changing norms, habits, skills and beliefs', and the enduring and
inevitable relative autonomy of teachers means that there will always be a varying
balance across the system between imposed structural changes and teacher agency,
mediated through the dominant cultures of teaching. In some contexts, structural
changes will prevail, whilst in others the key factor will be the active agency of teachers.
Thus the nature and extent of teacher 'professionalism' will continue to be contested
and redefined through the infinite number of choices made within individual schools

and classrooms. It is these choices which, cumulatively, shape both the experience of teaching and the outcomes of any educational reform initiatives.

Some evidence of the impact of the whole set of educational reforms upon teachers' sense of professionalism, and of the way that this can change over time, comes from interviews conducted as part of the PCT study. Prompt 8 (about recent changes to teaching and to teacher professionalism) elicited comments from the majority of respondents about greatly increased pressure and workloads. About a half of the group spontaneously made some comment about the excessive amount of change that they had experienced, whilst about one in three specifically mentioned the additional administrative and bureaucratic requirements, especially in terms of paperwork, that had been imposed upon them. It is difficult to be precise about these proportions since, as we have already indicated, this particular question was open-ended and elicited fairly naturalistic responses. However, this adds further weight to the categories, since they reflect the aspects of change upon which substantial numbers of interviewees chose to comment. Sometimes people spoke of the increased time pressures and the way in which work demands now intruded upon people's personal lives, sometimes of the demoralizing and disorienting effects of multiple change:

> When you're up till all hours preparing documents for inspection and marking, your social life goes out the window.

> It's the fact that you're just starting to get on your feet with one thing and you find that you've got a whole new change introduced and you've got to change everything again.

> The chaos which has been imposed on schools in terms of reorganization, reorganizing the curriculum ... and everything coming at the same time, teaching days changing ... to a more frenetic pace.

Approximately one in three also highlighted the effects of recent changes in the student population, which had created a greater number of pastoral problems and meant that teachers often had to adopt the role of social worker, as well as dealing with disruption in class. A lack of resources meant that teaching accommodation was often inadequate, class sizes too large and teaching materials in short supply. Additional pressures were said to have been created by Ofsted inspections and by the publication of league tables of assessment results, whilst nearly one in four complained in general terms of the increased accountability. Nearly a third of interviewees commented on the bad press that teachers had received, despite the difficult conditions in which they were working, and on their perceived loss of public status.

In such trying circumstances, these teachers displayed varying reactions in terms both of their professional confidence and of their overall sense of professionalism. For some, this was clearly diminished by the excessive pressures and by external prescription:

> You know, don't you, what morale's like in schools, particularly? That's something to do with increased ... chaos, I think, in increased paperwork ... more and more people are feeling less professional in the sense that they say, 'Oh, why should I bother?'

> [The National Curriculum] makes me less professional in that it makes me not have to think as much sometimes. I don't have to put so much into it possibly ... if it is more prescriptive and I'm told what I've got to do.

In extreme cases, this led to stress-related illness or even breakdown:

We're increasingly aware that stress is a big problem in teaching ... people are taking time off, if you like, through illness, but it's illness that's brought on by the sheer weight of the work that they've got to do. Different people cope with it in different ways but yes, I think it's increasing.

I've been off long-term with illness, so I'm only just back in school. And it was burn-out. I was literally working all the time.

Others were adopting what they believed was a 'professional' approach in trying to keep up with the work, although admitting they were driven by a possibly misplaced sense of conscientiousness:

I do find it hard work. But there again, you see, there's always this old argument, there's nobody telling you to do it a lot of the time. [You do it] to get through the volume of work and, yes, because at the bottom line I like a job well done and I wouldn't be content myself if I felt I'd just dropped something and chosen not to do it, you know, I take my responsibilities quite seriously, I suppose too seriously.

One or two respondents, however, appeared to be thriving on the changes, felt confident about what they were doing and believed that their professionalism had been enhanced:

I actually think there's more imagination in teaching now ... maths teachers talk more about maths now than they ever did before.

I do feel that their professionalism has improved because ... they do have an aim and they do have good guidance in terms of what they have to deliver.

Interestingly, there was some evidence of a change of attitude towards the National Curriculum between the first and second sets of PCT interviews, with more negative comments in 1994–5 and a sense in the 1995–6 interviews of some teachers regaining confidence and beginning to reassert a degree of curriculum control. There were also, however, some suggestions that factors other than the National Curriculum were now impinging more strongly upon teachers' work and upon their sense of professionalism. Although we did not ask any specific questions about these areas, some teachers in the second round of interviews did make detailed and substantial comments on the increase in managerialism and the growing divide between teachers and teacher managers; on the sense of isolation arising from a lack of contact with LEA advisers or with teachers from other schools and/or from a lessening of sociability and collaboration within their own institution; on their inability to maintain high standards in the face of constant work overload; and on the demoralizing effects of Ofsted inspections. In each case, there was a strong suggestion that the changes were having an adverse effect upon teachers' professional confidence:

There doesn't seem to be a profession any more. We just seem to be so brow beaten, scurrying around, snatching those odd moments to say hello to our colleagues, then we're back into class.

You've got increased class size ... we're teaching a slightly heavier timetable and, you know, that has an adverse effect I think on the quality of your teaching ... We're the professionals, our job is to teach, and all I want is a resource to back that up and money is a real problem.

I think there's also a distinction beginning to emerge within teaching that perhaps people who occupy more senior posts ... can actually see themselves as professionals, whereas people who are actually doing the job see themselves very much as being driven by what's required of them, the whole thing is specified for them ... the sort of professionalism that is coming in to the top end of the teaching profession now is that of manager more than educationalist.

In more recent years the shortage of teachers in some secondary school subjects and the difficulties in attracting bright graduates into teaching have led to considerable mod-ification in the political discourses of derision, particularly since the advent of the new Labour government in 1997. Indeed, there is now much more talk of 'professional' teachers and of the important role that they play. One of the teachers in the PCT study identified a degree of paradox in the current situation:

> I feel, on the one hand, teachers are very much encouraged to go out and teach on their own to a class, to make decisions, think on their feet, and then the next minute ... you have to conform to all these new rules and regulations and pieces of paper, and I think there's a bit of a paradox there.

Certainly there is paradox apparent in some of the Labour education policies: for example the early decision to 'name and shame' so-called 'failing schools' contrasts with supportive tributes by ministers to the hard work and skill of teachers. Likewise, proposals for performance-related pay and for the creation of a fast-track route for promising young teachers necessarily have a degree of arbitrariness about them and will probably be divisive, motivating those who are rewarded but demoralizing others who are not. At the same time, talk of engaging teachers in consultation over future curriculum policies and the encouragement of experimentation in Education Action Zones contrasts, in primary schools at least, with heavy prescription over the literacy and numeracy hours. (This prescription does not break the 1988 ERA, since schools can ignore it, but they do so at the risk of being castigated by Ofsted.)

## TEACHING AS A PROFESSION

It is hard to face the evidence of repeated changes to teachers' work, especially but not only in Britain, without feeling that something has been lost. Teachers may never have had as much curriculum autonomy as the myths in currency in the 1960s and 1970s suggested but now even those myths are gone and there is some need to point to the exaggerations in the new myth that teachers have lost control of the curriculum.

At the same time, managerialism, accountability, persistently unimpresssive levels of pay, discourses of derision, and the *de facto* prescription of primary school pedagogies in the literacy and numeracy hours all combine to erode notions that teaching is a profession. It is not surprising that commentators add to this the observations that teachers are working longer and harder and on tasks that are not usually their source of psychic rewards (especially bureaucratic meetings, record-keeping and other paper-work) and conclude that teaching is being deprofessionalized and proletarianized.

An alternative view is that professions in general are changing, and that evidence of this can be seen across the world. In some respects occupations such as teaching are becoming more professional, as new skills are required, achieving good relationships with clients and other stakeholders becomes more important, a more extensive knowledge-base has to be mastered and more complex decisions need to be made. Rather than being deprofessionalized, it could be argued that teaching is being reprofessionalized, although the new professionalism is different from the mythical professionalism of forty years ago. In England, years in which discourse about teachers has been derisive to the point that a leading Conservative politician said in 1999 that the teaching profession had become lost territory to his party, are being followed by signs of mollification.

This 'new professionalism' may have to be something more than conciliation, image-boosting and a recognition of the skill needed to work in new educational structures. The ways of working that were identified with organizational learning in the last chapter are also ways of working that researchers into organizational effectiveness identify as critical for success in times when continuous quality improvement is necessary. Looking at how teachers will need to work if schools are to be high-trust organizations, it is possible to suggest that we need to go beyond the limited view of 'new professionalism' contained in the English consultative document of late 1998 (DfEE 1998). These are themes pervading the next and final chapter.

# Chapter 8

# Conclusions: Towards a New Professionalism?

This work has explored changing attitudes towards teacher professionalism with regard to secondary school teachers in England over the past half-century. It has focused in particular on the complex political characteristics of teacher professionalism, not necessarily party political or overtly ideological in nature but nonetheless involving continual debate and negotiation. At the foreground has been the received image of teacher professionalism, the 'English tradition', a myth that assumed such an imposing form in the 1950s and 1960s. This has undergone both constant erosion from without and seismic convulsions from within, to such effect that its profile was both reduced and transformed. And yet, as we have seen, ideas about teacher professionalism remained important and influential. First, the myths and memories attached to the older professionalism proved to have considerable residual power, even growing in their talismanic significance when set against contemporary innovations. They were sufficient indeed to continue to shape the thinking of teachers, and often to constrain and limit the ambitions of new policy initiatives including the National Curriculum. Second, into the gap left by the progressive decline of this older professionalism poured new ideas and precepts, often incoherent and inconsistent, which jostled with each other and against older ideals in the process of forging a recognizably new professionalism.

The 'modernised professionalism' celebrated in the 1998 Green Paper *Teachers: Meeting the Challenge of Change* was no longer based on teacher control in the curriculum domain, as teacher professionalism had been thirty years before. Indeed, the Green Paper explicitly turned its face against this earlier ideal as it insisted categorically that 'The time has long gone when isolated, unaccountable professionals made curriculum and pedagogical decisions alone, without reference to the outside world' (DfEE 1998, p. 14). The review of the National Curriculum during 1999 reflected some continued concern for 'professional discretion'. For example, Blunkett observed that teachers 'should have more scope to use their professional discretion during key stage 3 to teach topics in depth', although he added at the same time that 'it is of course important that youngsters have a grounding in British history and Shakespeare for example' (Blunkett 1999). Continuities remained highly significant in the midst of change. Nevertheless, important arguments had been lost and won since the Dearing review of five or six years before, and the debate had moved on.

An analysis of the making of curriculum in American schools (Kliebard 1987) argues that in the twentieth century four main sets of ideas have been continually combining in different ways and with different force, so that at one point one idea appeared dominant to be later supplanted by another. All of the ideas had some support throughout the period. Lawton (1993) has said something similar about curriculum in Britain, arguing that national policy is the outcome of the political interplay amongst four interest groups. As far as the standing of teaching is concerned, there are probably no new myths, only ones that are favoured or rejected at any time. Policy oscillates between trust and mistrust, between control and subsidiarity, between simple, common-sense thinking and complex explorations, and between collaboration and confrontation.

A compelling point in Chapter 3 is that realities are more complex than is implied by the assumptions embedded in the competing discourses about policy. Teachers did not have as much control of the curriculum in the 1960s and 1970s as was proclaimed. Equally, the National Curriculum has not totally stripped away their control of the curriculum, nor can the changes of the past fifteen years be taken as plain evidence of deprofessionalization. Changes to teachers' conditions of work are variously constructed, as indicated in Chapter 7. Teachers' age, gender, work experience, teaching subject, departmental culture, career stage and ambitions, the school ethos, their teaching schedule, and their personal and professional confidence are but some of the factors that affect the ways in which meanings are attributed to changes in the objective conditions of work. Halford and Leonard (1999), writing of changes in the public sector in general, have argued that the impact of changes on workers' self-identity cannot be simply predicted, since the changes are given meanings and force by the people affected by them. Change and effect are not in a linear relationship.

On the other hand, objective aspects of public-sector work have undoubtedly changed. It is not only in England that governments have given priority to some, if not all of the changes that have affected teachers' occupational status. These have included market liberalization and reduction of barriers to competition; emphasis on market and quasi-market mechanisms for resource allocation; a diminution of the state's role as a guarantor of equity in welfare provision, so that some schools can effectively select 'privileged' children, while others become 'sink' schools; reduction in the unit cost of welfare provision, including education spending; and parsimony in the pay of 'welfare professionals'. At the same time demands for enhancement of service quality as measured by performance indicators have grown, together with closer specification of service quality, achieved by tight product specification (as with the National Curriculum), more stringent quality control (Ofsted, league tables, 'naming and shaming'), and remediation of producers with high defect rates (putting schools under 'special measures', exploring the privatization of failing schools), and closer specification of service processes, as in the *de facto* control of the pedagogy of the literacy and numeracy hours in British primary schools. These developments have encouraged a reduced regard for the professional value of providing the best service for a client, regardless of cost (most obvious in health care, where treatment is often related to funding). They have also fed a discourse about professionalism that imputes deficiencies in service delivery to professional dereliction – the individualization of problems that are often largely structural problems outside professionals' reach. Such a discourse expects improvements in service quality to be achieved through individuals being over-conscientious and attempts to colonize the affective domain so that people feel it is right to be public-sector Stakhanovites or workaholics (Willmott 1993). It produces in turn standardized professional training and commodified, on-the-job retraining (as opposed to in-service education and professional learning), and the growing employment of supposedly more biddable and more flexible females as low pay inclines men, who often see themselves as 'breadwinners', to other economic sectors.

All of this could be read as convincing evidence that it would be better to speak of proletarianization rather than of new professionalism. Yet, following the view that at any one time there are myths, realities and perspectives that exist and compete with one another, it is necessary to note problems with the proletarianization thesis. First, the absence of an agreed baseline or definition of a profession makes it unclear what is being compared with what. Choose different baselines and different views of deprofessionalization automatically follow. Second, the changes described above are affecting all professions to a greater or lesser degree, and not only professions in Britain. The corollary is that we ought to talk of 'the end of professions', not just of the deprofessionalization of teaching. In Sir William Taylor's words,

> the debate on professionalism has moved on. Neither the language nor the agenda are those of the 1970s ... Those who pin their hopes on an eventual change in the political climate must reckon with the possibility that both the language and the agenda have changed in ways that are irreversible.                    (Taylor 1994, pp. 57–8)

Third, in welfare systems, the delivery of services is heavily contingent (on the client, the client's problem and ecological features). Furthermore, policies, guidelines and criteria are ambiguous and are attributed different meanings by different practitioners. The consequence is that there are limits to the potential standardization and commodification of service delivery. Delivery remains substantially in the purview of the practitioners, individually and as groups. Consequently, welfare organizations are, in many regards, 'loose-coupled' systems. Much of their work cannot be routinized, unambiguously specified or readily measured. Non-routine, individual, values-shaped decision-making – professional judgement – is central to their activities.

Requirements of some of the innovations, notably the National Curriculum, imply that teachers have to acquire more knowledge, display a wide range of pedagogic skills, make more, high-inference judgements, and interact more with other adults. There are suggestions – no more – that objections to these changes come primarily from those who worked in the rather different, pre-change systems. Comparisons with other educational systems and hints from those teachers who have just started their careers might be indicating that ascriptions of deprofessionalization are signs that older teachers are *en recherche du temps perdu*. That does not mean that the changes are any the less stressful (Lazarus 1991). It does imply that judgements about the meaning of those changes should be circumspect, especially as teachers seem to be acclimatizing to elements of the new environment and finding spaces for their own expressions of educational worth. However, this is a line that needs to be properly researched in a variety of public-sector settings.

It is arguable whether teaching in Britain is becoming proletarianized. Whatever the preferred answer, a striking consequence of the changes that have made these definitional matters cause for concern is that 'teachers are Britain's unhappiest workers'. A report in *The Guardian* of 15 March 1999 said that interviews with 7000 public-sector workers had established that teachers had 'much lower levels of job satisfaction than other public or even private sector workers'.

Yet, there is talk of 'new professionalism'. An international conference on this theme in Hong Kong in 1999 showed that there are many meanings attached to this seductive term. For example, Caldwell (1999) explored the implications of creating world-class schools for the third millennium, which patently required teaching professionals; Sachs (1999) argued for the development of an 'activist view' of professionalism; and Goodson (1999) proposed a set of six meanings for new professionalism, namely:

- increased opportunity and responsibility to exercise discretionary judgement over issues of teaching, curriculum and care ...
- commitment to working with colleagues in collaborative cultures of shared expertise ...
- ... teachers work authoritatively yet openly with other partners in the wider community ...
- a commitment to active *care* and not just anodyne *service* for students ...
- a self-directed search and struggle for *continuous learning* ... rather than compliance with the enervating obligations of *endless change* ...
- the creation and recognition of high task *complexity* ...

Hargreaves (1999b) emphasized the importance of working with parents and the wider community, arguing that 'if teachers want to become professionally stronger, they must now open themselves up and become more publicly vulnerable and accessible. That is their paradoxical challenge in the postmodern age'. He also (1999a) developed an earlier theme about the significance of the emotions in professionals' work.

Clearly, understandings of the term 'new professionalism' rest upon understandings of 'old professionalism' in any country or context, as well as upon the goals and beliefs of the people using the term. It is a term of implied approval that only has meaning in a context. With that in mind, we examine it in the setting of thinking about British teachers' occupational status.

The 1998 Green Paper (DfEE 1998) begins by saying that government aims for the profession are ' ... higher status, better prospects, a rewarding career structure, less bureaucracy, more freedom to focus on teaching, a new professionalism, greater individual accountability, more flexibility and higher standards' (p. 13).

Developing this theme, the chief executive of the Teacher Training Agency said that,

> a new professionalism is developing amongst our teachers but ... it needs a significant boost from all sides – Ministers, LEAs, the press, parents and, most important, from teachers themselves if we are to ensure that teachers' self-image and self confidence improve sufficiently for teaching to become an attractive career option in the next century.
>
> (Millett 1999a)

At face value these proposals address some of the things that have undermined teachers' job satisfaction. They also promise more money for some:

> access to higher pay for teachers with consistently strong performance; a School Performance Award Scheme to reward achievement by whole schools; ... more pay for tough headship jobs; [and] a national fast-track scheme to help talented trainees and teachers advance rapidly. (DfEE 1998, pp. 12–13)

Anthea Millett's speech on the new professionalism also contained many up-beat points, such as the need to improve the work environment so that '[T]he squabbles over the milk, the beaten-up armchairs and the wholly inadequate access to working space, which still characterise many of our staffrooms, must go.' But it also echoed another, familiar discourse of control, emphasizing that teachers had to concentrate on delivering 'literacy, numeracy and information technology' and to make better use 'of inspection and research evidence to inform their practice in the classroom'. In another speech on the same day she combined support and control:

> we shall see substantial Continuing Professional Development expenditure of some £600 million per annum available ... [But] we must see fewer familiarisation courses on the trendy topic of the moment.                                            (Millett 1999b)

In the Green Paper the old language of accountability lay alongside attempts to raise morale, so there were to be

> appraisal of teachers' performance as the basis for professional judgements on pay and career development; ... option of fixed-term contracts, and more effective appraisal arrangements for heads.                                   (DfEE 1998, pp. 12–13)

Teacher unions have reacted to that with hostility. Their main objections were that it is impossible to set fair performance targets linked to the award of performance-related pay (PRP). Different teachers doing different jobs with different pupils in different schools pose insurmountable problems to the idea of a transparently fair PRP system. There is also the old danger of 'putting [children] under pressure to achieve good test scores to boost teachers' earnings. "Play will disappear altogether" [foresaw one teacher] "Children will be taught about commas instead of being allowed to play in the sand tray"' (*The Guardian*, 5 April 1999, p. 6). Questions arise about who will do the appraisal with one teacher fearing that 'if you don't get on with the headteacher you are well and truly stuffed' (*The Guardian*, 30 March 1999, p. 4). Some evidence has been seen that divisions are appearing in secondary schools between management teams and other teachers and there are suspicions that managers and 'whiz-kids' will benefit from PRP, to the detriment of the team spirit and collegiality that are said to be vital to effective schooling (*The Guardian*, 30 March 1999, p. 4). If these fears show a government feeling that professionals need to be controlled, monitored and managed if they are to perform well and unions that are alert to the downsides of change, then two further aspects of PRP highlight the different stances on professionalism.

The Green Paper said that teachers qualifying for PRP would have to accept new contracts that required them to work unspecified hours. Since existing contracts oblige teachers to work 1265 hours a year under the direction of the headteacher, it appears that government intends to make teachers on PRP work much harder. Yet this requirement seems to be unnecessary on two grounds. The first is the consistent finding that teachers work well over 1265 hours a year (Campbell and Neill 1994b), something that is borne out by the remarks of teachers we interviewed. Second, it is very hard to see how a teacher would qualify for PRP without considerable devotion to duty. The proposal would simply put into contractual form what the majority of teachers do already. Why? An easy conclusion to draw is that it indicates official mistrust of teachers, who are reckoned to be professional to the extent to which they can be compelled to be professional.

The history of PRP in the civil service, where all pay awards since 1992 have been performance-related, shows that the link between performance and rewards is constrained by cash limits. In 1998 people whose performance was judged satisfactory or better received awards that barely kept pace with inflation (Letter from Paul Noon, *The Guardian*, 12 April 1999). Teacher PRP would also be cash limited and the ceiling of £35,000, compared to an existing rate of £22,400, would be available only to a few. In other words, PRP would do nothing to enhance the pay of the majority of teachers. It would allow the claim that classroom teaching offers fairly-glittering prizes and obscure the fact that most classroom teachers would continue to receive a distinctly run-of-the mill salary for graduate, non-manual work. PRP could be seen as a piece of spin-doctoring, not as a serious attempt to improve the professional standing of teaching. In Sweden, said a report in *The Guardian* of 8 May 1999, PRP for teachers has been 'an unmitigated disaster, causing untold strife and not much in the way of educational improvement'.

Mistrust is at the heart of British government thinking about new professionalism and of teachers' reactions to government policies. In an article in *The Independent on Sunday* (11 April 1999) Michael McMahon explained why he was retiring from teaching in a 'failing' inner-city high school. It was not so much the students, he explained, as the politicians, forever hindering his attempts to teach, by control, bureaucracy and inter-ference. Furthermore, what they expected and tried to get the school to do were unrealistic given the problems in the local environment that filled the school with difficulties. In a similar vein Gewirtz (1998) argued that some schools just cannot become more effective because of the suffocating pressures of merely coping, a theme also raised by a study of different school improvement trajectories (Gray *et al.* 1999). Government attempts to improve schooling appear, from these perspectives, to be more than by-passing the professionals; they appear to be preventing the teachers from acting professionally. Andy Hargreaves has made a related point saying that 'without attention to the [teachers'] emotions, educational reform efforts may ignore and even damage some of the most fundamental aspects of what teachers do' (1998 p. 850).

It remains to be seen how the politics of teacher professionalism will be played out in the future. Control of curriculum content may or may not be the central field of contestation. Fergusson (1994) has suggested that the introduction of a managerialist system into schools, if successfully accomplished, will have more impact upon the centralization of power than any other current reforms, since it will serve as an effective conduit for whatever future measures the government of the day wishes to introduce. The evidence to date suggests that a teacher-proof system remains a chimera and that teachers, both individually and as a group, will necessarily continue to play an active part in creating educational reality within the changing frameworks. Indeed, it is highly unlikely that the work of teaching can ever be reduced to a mechanistic activity within a tight-coupled system. As long as the implementation of policy requires customization to specific circumstances, and as long as classroom teaching is a matter of non-routine decision-making that is contexted, specific, interactive and – to some extent – intuitive, it is hard to see that education can ever be 'teacher-proofed' and thereby depro-fessionalized.

But it is arguable that what matters most is not whether the case can be developed that teaching has many, perhaps most, of the traits of a profession. What matters most may be the way teachers are regarded by governments and by the community. Evidence about teachers' standing in the community is hard to come by but the evidence of the 1998 British Green Paper is that politicians do not trust teachers. What may matter more is the way teachers see themselves. For sure, many teachers have learnt to cope with government mandates and this experience may have strengthened their confidence and enhanced their skills. But do teachers feel themselves to be valued, appreciated and trusted? Are they fulfilled in their work? We may examine the politics of professionalism, notice the cross-currents of myths and appreciate the different arguments about whether teaching is a profession or not and still miss an important point. If, by and large, teachers do not feel fulfilled in their work, trusted and valued; if they do not *feel* professional, then can teaching really be seen as a profession?

The question is an important one because the improvements that governments want cannot be mandated. They depend on teachers going beyond what is prescribed and working within the spirit of *kaizen* (continuous quality improvement), whether they take the path of action research, tinkering with the curriculum, the development of collegiality, or of attention to the processes of classroom learning and teaching. Educational improvement depends on teachers wanting to make a difference. It depends upon their feeling professional. Neither raising standards by regulation nor professionalizing by prescription will work. Teachers have power in the sense that they have to want improvement for improvement to happen.

The social psychologist Martin Seligman has drawn attention to the way in which some people respond to the social structures and events with learned helplessness while others respond to the same things with learned optimism (1998). People make themselves victims or capable agents in some degree according to the ways in which they interpret what happens and respond to it. The structures within which teachers work may not be those we would wish. However, the ways in which teachers respond to structures and changes – the extent to which they assert their agency and demonstrate 'learned optimism', by creating spaces, taking initiatives, making partnerships, proclaiming their work and achievements – have a great deal to do with the standing of teaching as an occupation.

There has been a tendency for teachers to cast themselves as victims of malign structural forces, a portrait favoured by other groups as well. There is an alternative. The politics of professionalism are partly about government actions that affect teachers but they are also about the ways in which teachers choose to respond and choose to publicly depict themselves. Discussions of 'new professionalism', as well as of 'old professionalism', show that there is a choice.

And where there is a choice, there is also challenge and the prospect of change. The version of 'new professionalism' presented in the 1998 Green Paper resembles nothing so much as an officially approved package. Alternatives are not only possible but are likely to develop alongside and in opposition to this. Even in a situation where there is broad outward agreement, as was found in the 1950s and 1960s, there is scope for differences and negotiation. If negotiation founders and open conflict ensues, as in the 1980s, different principles may emerge to constitute a new myth of teacher professionalism. For all the influence and resources of its progenitors, 'modernized professionalism' may itself have only a limited shelf-life. It could indeed be as transitory as previous forms of teacher professionalism and perhaps more so. Blunkett, Millett and Woodhead may come to appear as outdated in their common-sense assumptions in twenty years' time as Eccles, Clegg and Kerr do today. Whether or not this proves to be the case, teacher professionalism will continue to be contested as it has been over the past fifty years and more. The politics of professionalism has far from run its course.

# Appendix: The Professional Cultures of Teachers Project

The table overleaf summarizes the investigation of teachers' professional cultures through interviews and questionnaires involving 178 teachers in north-west England between late 1994 and early 1996. At that point the National Curriculum had operated for four years (five in the case of mathematics), although revisions came into force in September 1995. The views of thirteen 'key informants' were also solicited in the summer of 1995 to give snapshots of the ground as seen from within the policy community. In addition, historical studies were carried out to set this survey work in perspective; there was a study of the way that teaching cultures were represented in the press at a point (1976) where the claim that teaching is a profession was vigorously contested; views of teacher professionalism in the educational press were studied for five significant points, namely 1965, 1976, 1983, 1987 and 1993; and there was an investigation of the ways in which subject associations, such as those covering home economics and geography, shaped and defended the professional cultures of teachers as teachers of mathematics, history, geography and technology in the period 1976–95 (Knight 1996).

Observational and experimental methods were quickly rejected as unsuitable for a study of teachers' thinking and beliefs. Questionnaires were not seen as useful for exploring the depth and complexity of beliefs. It was also feared that they would tend to lead informants to describe their understandings in ways that lay close to the questions, effectively masking things that were not covered by the questions. Nevertheless, two questionnaires were used, each designed to capture essentially unambiguous information.

The flexibility and interpersonal nature of interviews was thought to make this less likely, although it was recognized that in all research the uneven distribution of power between the researcher and the informant can lead to results that are contaminated by informants following the lines set out by the researcher. Telephone interviewing is not considered to be a good way of conducting exploratory interviews such as these (Arksey and Knight 1999). There was also a practical problem of contacting individuals by phone: it is difficult to do at work (and even more difficult for teachers to talk privately from school) and the team neither had, nor thought it should have, access to teachers' home phone numbers.

Summary of PCT interview and questionnaire research.

| Interviews | Questionnaire | Analysis |
|---|---|---|
| Interview prompts discussed and repeatedly revised. Then piloted on ten teachers and revised again. | Questionnaire 1 piloted on ten teachers and revised. | Impressionistic reading of all data by all five researchers to check for quality of responses to interview and questionnaire schedules. |
| Interviews with 178 secondary school teachers, shared between the five researchers. Modal length = 35 minutes. Range = 20 minutes to 60 minutes+. Sample comprises equal numbers of volunteer classroom teachers of maths, technology and humanities. More or less equal balance of men and women from the north-west of England and Sheffield. | Questionnaire 1 sent to teachers before the interview and collected at the end of the interview. | Interviews transcribed and circulated to all five researchers. Reactions to the interviews discussed and working understandings of the data emerge. Questionnaire 1 is analytically unproblematic, containing fixed-response answers. Entered on to computer and summarized through SPSS+ software |
| | Questionnaire 2 developed, piloted, discussed and given to teachers at the end of the interview (mailed to those interviewed early in the research). | Two people independently review answers to two of the main prompts on the schedule and report back to the group. Discussion of the meanings and interpretations. Re-analysis of data. Agreement on plausibility of re-analyses. |
| Second interviews with a sample of 32 of the 178 teachers chosen on the grounds that they had interesting things to say – not for their 'representativeness'. Their prompts were intended to develop and clarify themes that were emerging from the analysis of the first round of interviews. | | Interview reports (summaries) read by all and analysed by two people who were trying to construct plausible interpretations of the data that were then put before the full research team for appraisal. |
| Interviews with thirteen key informants – policy-makers, senior officials, politicians. We had identified 35 people who we thought might be good key informants. Their prompts were intended to develop and clarify themes that were emerging from the analysis of the first round of interviews. | | Questionnaire 2 analysed. Content analysis used to generate main categories of response. Review by all researchers of findings. Interviews transcribed, checked and discussed. Data used to supplement and triangulate the picture that has emerged from the questionnaires and interview reports. |

For these reasons, face-to-face interviewing was selected as the main research method, despite the considerable time, travel and transcription costs, and in the knowledge that the data would be hard to analyse. A typical interview ranged from 35 minutes to an hour and took up ten pages of close-typed transcript.

## The interviews

The main interview schedule that was used was the fifth draft and was based on three principles. First, that there should be few topics of discussion, so as to allow informants to develop their views at length. Second, that the information of greatest interest would be that at 'the front of the mind' – that which was spontaneously volunteered. There would be many aspects of the professional nature of teachers' work that might not be volunteered and on which the teachers could talk, if prompted. However, our interest was in the information that teachers felt to be salient enough to volunteer without interviewer guidance. Third, the interview schedule had to avoid assuming something that was to be investigated, namely whether teaching *is* a profession. For this reason a 'progressive focus' structure was adopted. First teachers were asked to talk about professions in general. They were then asked whether teaching fitted the account of a profession that they had volunteered, and, by implication, to say whether teaching was, in their view, a profession. Thence they were asked to identify aspects of their work that they saw as professional when they were working as a subject teacher, and again when they were working in a different role, which was usually in a pastoral role. All in all, the interview prompts were designed to allow informants to explain in depth what, if anything, made teaching a profession for them; how their work showed these professional characteristics in action; and how the professional nature of their work had changed, if at all. Further discussion of this approach to interviewing is in Knight and Saunders (1999).

Thirty-two of the teachers agreed to be interviewed a second time. The intention was to investigate themes that had emerged from the first round of interviews, checking and extending the researchers' understanding. The sample was definitely not chosen to be representative. Writing of sampling in qualitative interviews, Rubin and Rubin (1995) advocate choosing informants on the basis of their power to illuminate issues, not because they are representative. That was the procedure followed here. Each member of the research team nominated teachers who they had interviewed and who had seemed to be especially forthcoming, to have interesting or unusual points of view, or to have well-developed ideas. The final selection was made with an eye to trying to achieve a balanced representation of male and female teachers, and produced a list of 34 (the target was 30), of whom 32 were interviewed.

Key informants' views help sketch a context in which the teachers' perspectives can be located. Their understandings were not solicited in order to check the validity of the teachers' accounts but to show the degree to which the classroom teachers' understandings of their professional cultures were shared by some of those with a different perspective on schooling. They were intended to be complementary, not validating. Thirteen interviews were done with key informants.

## Reliability issues

In many ways, the concept of a reliable interview is most appropriate where a fixed-response interview schedule is used. In those cases, interviewers can be trained to all read exactly the same questions in the same sequence and to deal with respondents' incomprehension, silence or questions in virtually the same ways. A good example is telephone interviewing, where interviewers' behaviours are closely monitored and deviations from the agreed script can be swiftly dealt with. However, when the purpose is to explore meanings, rather than to survey the extent to which people agree with the researchers' questions and response categories, then the notion of reliability becomes far more problematic. Interviewers will use different ways to build trust and to encourage informants to 'open up'. Because they wish to learn about the world as informants see it, they will need to use their judgement in reacting to complex and not-always-clear answers to their questions. In a sense, reliability is not an appropriate concept here. Reliable interviews are similar interviews, whereas these semi-structured interviews took paths that were to a greater or lesser extent unpredictable.

The case should not be overstated, since all five interviewers had collaborated in producing the schedule and all hoped to use the nine prompts in the progressive focusing sequence that had been agreed. Yet, it was common to find informants mingling discussions of professions in general with their views on the professional nature of teaching; to describe changes in their work throughout the interview; and to revise their earlier answers when explaining what made one teacher more professional than another. Furthermore, there were differences in the interviewers' natural styles. Some frequently asked for clarification, prompted and asked questions, while others tried to stay as quiet as possible. These differences were discussed and some convergence of practice was achieved, subject always to the goal of getting the best expression of teachers' thinking about the professional nature of their work.

These interviews were reliable only in the sense that in each case informants were invited to talk at length about what they had in mind in response to our nine prompt questions. Giving priority to validity – to hearing the teachers' voices – over reliability has an important consequence for external validity. Just because an informant did not say something, it does not mean that they were unaware of that point or unable to talk about it. All that can be said is that the way the interview played out meant that the point was not spontaneously made at that time in that specific setting. At another time, in another interview, the point might have been made. By contrast, highly structured surveys, such as telephone interviews, are designed to probe respondents' receptive understanding – their response to the detailed questions and response categories – in ways that are reliable in the sense that the same answers are very likely to be given by the same respondents on different occasions. Because these interviews did not exhaustively probe informants' receptive understanding but concentrated on their spontaneous, front-of-the-mind thinking, it is impossible to generalize from them. It cannot be said that 33 per cent of informants thought that a defining feature of a profession was that it involved sustained education and knowledge-acquisition. The most that can be said is that 33 per cent of informants spontaneously volunteered that point. Whether the other 67 per cent would have agreed, had they been given the option of nominating this characteristic in a structured survey-type interview, cannot be known. As a consequence, it was futile to use sophisticated statistical methods to describe the responses.

Our data describe only what these people volunteered. It cannot easily be said that it represents the extent of their understandings, nor can generalizations be made about the likely responses of a different set of informants. The external validity of the interviews is, formally, limited by the lack of reliability.

Interviews were taped and the interviewer produced a summary of the interview in note form that was circulated to all five investigators as soon as possible after the interview. (Only in the pilot interviews and two key informant interviews were two interviewers present.) As far as possible, full transcripts of the interview followed, but it was sometimes necessary to transcribe only parts of an interview or not to transcribe interviews that the interviewer judged to make routine points in routine ways: the tape record was always available for reference. This process meant that all members of the team were constantly reading accounts of interviews and beginning to see for themselves categories of analysis. These emergent and sometimes distinct understandings were discussed at team meetings, with the result that when full-scale analysis of the data was begun, it was partly on the basis of the implicit analysis that had been taking place as the team interviewed and read accounts of interviews.

The analysis of the 178 interviews was a long, vexed and uncertain activity. The first approach to reviewing the complete set was to have one member of the research team read through a sample of responses that could be related to one of the nine lead questions. Reports on this initial, impressionistic analysis were presented to the team and discussed, with each member setting alongside it her or his understanding of the data that had been formed as interview accounts had been circulated and interviews conducted. Discussion indicated the lines of analysis that seemed to be the most valid and acceptable to the five investigators.

This is a familiar analytical approach in qualitative research (Arksey and Knight 1999). The meanings emerge as the data are read and re-read. Interpretations of what the data mean are ventured, discussed, defended and often modified. The analytical categories that are left are then applied to a further reading of the data. They may embrace most of the data, or further modifications may be needed to get a good fit between the analytical categories that make sense to the researcher and the words of the informants.

Pairs of investigators then independently analysed all of the responses that could be associated with a lead question. The pairings differed for each of the nine questions, so that each researcher worked in two or three different coding pairs. This is always a complex task, since analysts frequently have to make high-inference judgements about the meaning of utterances and about which analytical category they seem to support. Moreover, an interviewing style that tended to follow the informants' lead, rather than to force them to confine themselves to the topic suggested by the researchers' questions, meant that responses which could be seen as relevant to any of the nine prompts could appear anywhere in the interview transcript. So, not only were there the well-known problems of assigning meaning to the data, but there were also difficulties in deciding what could be counted as data that bore upon a particular line of enquiry.

In one sense it was reassuring to see that where members of the research team had tried to tally the number of different ideas informants used in responding to a given prompt, they ended up with very similar counts. At the very least, it made it possible to say that teachers more frequently spontaneously used one set of concepts than another.

The snag was that the two researchers who analysed responses to each question may have agreed on the overall picture and differed quite sharply on some individual cases. If there was inter-observer reliability in this analysis – and there was – it was overall reliability obtained because disagreements about individual cases tended to cancel each other out.

At that point we abandoned the classic, psychometric notion of inter-observer reliability. For sure, it would have been possible to define the meanings of analytical categories more and more closely and to continually talk through the analyses until agreement was reached on every detail. All the resultant high inter-observer reliability would have proved was that two people could work together to form agreed inter-pretations of complex data. Even had the process been extended to bring five minds to bear on all prompts, it would still only have shown that five people could agree on an analysis if they worked long enough on it.

In the face of these realizations, we began to treat the interview accounts rather like a historical archive and to see their analyses as akin to the work of historians. Even if one does not accept the relativism of Carr's classic account of historians' work (1961), it is still clear that historians are steeped in working with data that are incomplete, biased and produced for a purpose; and in interpreting it in the light of their own questions and concerns, influenced by their understandings of previous work in the field. While there is often substantial agreement, there is also substantial disagreement about the best reading of a historical archive, disagreement that is not, usually, fuelled by one historian discovering sources that were previously unknown. This is not to suggest that history is an exercise in unbridled subjectivity. There are well-known rules of procedure (for example, the historian should cover all the relevant sources and be alert to the bias inherent in each) that impose a rigour on the process of interpretation. Nevertheless, readings differ, and one of the aims of historical scholarship is to displace an accepted reading with a better one: and what counts as better changes with time and according to the culture within which the historian works. The test of the adequacy of an interpretation is the extent to which it is plausible, accepted by other professionals, and is recognizable as a fair reading of the archive. It was this concept of reliability as plausibility that was applied to the interpretation of this large archive of interview material.

The claim is *not* that our readings of the interview data are the only readings. It is, rather, that these are readings that are plausible, that make sense to five people who have been immersed in the data, and that can be defended by reference to it. And, as has been said previously, these are interpretations that resonate with others working in the field.

# References

(Unpublished papers of the Ministry of Education and the Department of Education and Science are based at the Public Record Office, Kew, London.)

Acker, S. (1990) 'Teachers' culture in an English primary school: continuity and change', *British Journal of Sociology of Education*, **11**(3), 257–73.
Ackland, J. (1992) 'The National Curriculum and teachers' professional knowledge', in *The National Curriculum in Practice*, Perspectives 46. School of Education, University of Exeter.
Alexander, R. J. (1991) *Policy and Practice in Primary Education*. London: Routledge.
Allee, V. (1997) *The Knowledge Evolution*. Boston, MA: Butterworth-Heinemann.
Anderson, R. D. (1983) *Education and Opportunity in Victorian Scotland: Schools and Universities*. Edinburgh: Edinburgh University Press.
Apple, M. W. (1986) *Teachers and Texts: A Political Economy of Class and Gender Relations in Education*. New York: Routledge and Kegan Paul.
Apple, M. W. (1993) 'Whose curriculum is this anyway?', in M. Apple, *Official Knowledge*. London: Routledge.
Argyris, C. (1985) *Action Science*. San Francisco, CA: Jossey-Bass.
Arksey, H. and Knight, P. T. (1999) *Interviewing for Social Scientists*. London: Sage.
Badaracco, J. L. and Ellsworth, R. R. (1989) *Leadership and the Quest for Integrity*. Boston, MA: Harvard Business School Press.
Baker, K. (1993) *The Turbulent Years: My Life In Politics*. London: Faber and Faber.
Ball, S. (1990) *Politics and Policy Making in Education*. London: Routledge.
Ball, S. (1994) *Education Reform: A Critical and Post-Structural Approach*. Buckingham: Open University Press.
Ball, S. and Bowe, R. (1992) 'Subject departments and the "implementation" of National Curriculum policy: an overview of the issues', *Journal of Curriculum Studies*, **24**(2), 97–115.
Barach, J. A and Eckhardt, D. R. (1996) *Leadership and the Job of the Executive*. Westport, CT: Quorum Books.
Becher, T. (1996) 'The learning professions', *Studies in Higher Education*, **21**(1), 43–55.
Beeby, C. E. (1989) 'Introduction', in W. Renwick, *Moving Targets: Six Essays On Educational Policy*. Wellington: New Zealand Council for Educational Research.
Ben-Peretz, M. (1995) *Learning from Experience: Memory and the Teacher's Account of Teaching*. Albany: SUNY Press.
Bernstein, B. (1971) 'On the classification and framing of educational knowledge', in M. F. D. Young (ed.), *Knowledge and Control: New Directions for the Sociology of Education*. London: Cassell.
Bessey, G. (1964) letter to L.W. Norwood, 29 April (Ministry of Education papers, ED.147/655).
Binns, A. L. (1946) report to Lancashire education committee, 'The Future of the Modern School', 11 November (Lancashire education committee papers, Preston local records office).
Blackler, F. (1993) 'Knowledge and the theory of organizations: organizations as activity systems and the reframing of management', *Journal of Management Studies*, **30**(6), 863–84.

Blackler, F. (1995) 'Knowledge, knowledge work and organizations: an overview and analysis', *Organization Studies*, **16**(6), 1021–46.

Blair, T. (1999) 'Quality is key to progress', *TES*, 4 June.

Blunkett, D. (1998) 'Professionalism is back at the very heart of teaching', *The Guardian*, Education Supplement, 7 April.

Blunkett, D. (1999) 'A curriculum for all seasons', *TES*, 26 March.

Board of Education (1926) *The Education of the Adolescent* (Hadow Report). London: HMSO.

Bolton, E. (1993) 'Imaginary gardens with real toads', in B. Simon and C. Chitty (eds), *Education Answers Back: Critical Responses to Government Policy*. London: Lawrence and Wishart.

Bottery, M. (1996) 'The challenge to professionals from the New Public Management: implications for the teaching profession', *Oxford Review of Education*, **22**(2), 179–97.

Bottery, M. (1998) *Professionals and Policy: Management Strategy in a Competitive World*. London: Cassell.

Bottery, M. and Wright, N. (1996) 'Co-operating in their own deprofessionalization?', *British Journal of Educational Studies*, **44**(1), 82–98.

Bowe, R. and Ball, S. with Gold, A. (1992) *Reforming Education and Changing Schools: Case Studies in Policy Sociology*. London: Routledge.

Boyle, E. (1963) memo, 'Proposed Schools Council for the Curriculum and Examinations', 13 May (Ministry of Education papers, ED.147/812).

Bradley, H., Conner, C. and Southworth, J. (eds) (1994) *Developing Teachers, Developing Schools*. London: David Fulton.

Braverman, H. (1974) *Labour and Monopoly Capital: The Deregulation of Work in the Twentieth Century*. London: Monthly Review Press.

Broad, S. T. (1959) letter to Beloe Committee, paper no. 8, 13 March (Ministry of Education papers, ED.147/307).

Broadfoot, P. and Osborn, M. with Gilly, M. and Paillet, A. (1988) 'What professional responsibility means to teachers: national contexts and classroom constraints', *British Journal of Sociology of Education*, **9**(3), 265–87.

Burrage, M. and Torstendahl, R. (eds) (1990) *Professions in Theory and History*. London: Sage.

Bush, T. (1997) 'Collegial models', in A. Harris, N. Bennett and A. Preedy (eds), *Organizational Effectiveness and Improvement in Education*. Buckingham: Open University Press.

Butt, R., Townsend, D. and Raymond, D. (1990) 'Bringing reform to life', *Cambridge Journal of Education*, **20**(3), 255–68.

Calderhead, J. (1984) *Teachers' Classroom Decision-Making*. London: Rinehard and Winston.

Caldwell, B. (1999) *The Status of the New Professional in Schools of the Third Millennium*. Paper presented to the international conference on New Professionalism in Teaching, Hong Kong, 15–17 January.

Campbell, R. J. and Neill, S. R. St. J. (1994a) *Primary Teachers at Work*. London: Routledge.

Campbell, R. J. and Neill, S. R. St. J. (1994b) *Secondary Teachers at Work*. London: Routledge.

Carr, E. H. (1961) *What is History?* London: Penguin.

Central Advisory Council for Education (1967) *Children and their Primary Schools*. London: HMSO.

Chapman, R. (1995) 'New to teaching', in J. Bell (ed.), *Teachers Talk about Teaching: Coping with Change in Turbulent Times*. Milton Keynes: Open University Press.

Checkland, P. (1981) *Systems Thinking, Systems Practice*. Chichester: John Wiley.

Checkland, P. and Scholes, J. (1990) *Soft Systems Methodology in Action*. Chichester: John Wiley.

Chitty, C. (1988) 'Central control of the school curriculum, 1944–87', *History of Education*, **17**(4), 321–34.

Chitty, C. (1989) *Towards a New Education System: The Victory of the New Right?*. London: Falmer.

Connell, R. W. (1985) *Teachers' Work*. London: George Allen and Unwin.

Cooper, C. L. and Payne, R. (1988) (eds) *Causes, Coping and Consequences of Stress at Work*. Chichester: John Wiley.

Cooper, R. K. and Sawaf, A. (1997) *Executive EQ*. London: Orion Business Books.

Crawford, K. (1996) 'A history of the right: the battle for control of National Curriculum history', *British Journal of Educational Studies*, **43**(4), 433–56.

Cunningham, P. (1992) 'Teachers' professional image and the press 1950–1990', *History of Education*, **21**(1), 37–56.

Curriculum Study Group (1963) working paper no. 5, 'The Curriculum Study Group' (Ministry of Education papers, ED.147/814).

Darling-Hammond, L. and Cobb, V. L. (1995) *Teacher Preparation and Professional Development in Member Countries*. Washington, DC: Government Printing Office.

Day, C. (1993) 'Reflection: a necessary but not sufficient condition for professional development', *British Educational Research Journal*, **19**(1), 83–93.

Day, C. (1997) 'In-service teacher education in Europe', *British Journal of In-Service Education*, **23**(1), 39–54.

Day, C., Fernandez, A., Hauge, T. and Muller, J. (eds) (1999) *The Life and Work of Teachers: International Perspectives in Changing Times*. London: Falmer.

Dearing, R. (1993) *The National Curriculum and its Assessment: Final Report*. London: School Curriculum and Assessment Council.

Dent, H. C. (1952) *Change in English Education: A Historical Survey*. London: University of London Press.

Department for Education (1989) *Mathematics in the National Curriculum*. London: HMSO.

Department for Education/Welsh Office (1992) *Choice and Diversity: A New Framework for Schools* (Cmnd 2021). London: HMSO.

Department for Education and Employment (1998) *Teachers: Meeting the Challenge of Change* (Cm 4164). London: Stationery Office.

Department of Education and Science (1964) Note of meeting on the reorganization of secondary education, 23 November (DES papers, ED.147/826).

Department of Education and Science (1965) Inspectorate secondary education panel (A2), 43rd meeting, 15–16 December, minute 1 (DES papers, ED.158/21).

Department of Education and Science (1979) Report on 4th Meeting of Schools Council Convocation, London, 11 December (Schools Council papers, Public Record Office, EJ.13/7).

Department of Education and Science (1985) *Better Schools* (Cmnd 9469). London: HMSO.

Department of Education and Science (1987) *The National Curriculum 5–16: A Consultation Document*. London: HMSO.

Department of Education and Science (1988) *Task Group on Assessment and Testing: A Report*. London: HMSO.

Department of Education and Science (1989) *The National Curriculum: From Policy to Practice*. London: HMSO.

Dubin, S. S. (1990) 'Maintaining competence through updating', in S. L. Willis and S. S. Dubin (eds), *Maintaining Professional Competence*. San Francisco: Jossey-Bass.

Easterby-Smith, M. (1997) 'Disciplines of organizational learning: contributions and critiques', *Human Relations*, **50**(9), 1085–1113.

Eccles, D. (1955) note, ' "The New Secondary Education", 1947', 3 January (Ministry of Education papers, ED.147/207).

Eisenmann, L. (1991) 'Teacher professionalism: a new analytical tool for the history of teachers', *Harvard Educational Review*, **61**(2), 215–24.

Eraut, M. (1994) *Developing Professional Knowledge and Competence*, London: Falmer.

Eraut, M. (1997) 'Perspectives on defining "The learning society" ', *Journal of Education Policy*, **12**(6), 551–58.

Evans, L. (1998) *Teacher Morale, Job Satisfaction and Motivation*. London: Paul Chapman.

Evetts, J. (1994a) *Becoming a Secondary Head Teacher*. London: Cassell.

Evetts, J. (1994b) 'The new headteacher: the changing work culture of secondary headship', *School Organisation*, **14**(1), 37–47.

Fergusson, R. (1994) 'Managerialism in education', in J. Clarke, A. Cochrane and E. McLaughlin (eds), *Managing Social Policy*. London: Sage.

Fisher, S. (1994) *Stress in Academic Life*. Buckingham: Open University Press.

Freidson, E. (1970) *Profession of Medicine: A Study of the Sociology of Applied Knowledge*. New York: Harper and Row.

Freidson, E. (1994) *Professionalism Reborn: Theory, Prophecy and Policy*. Cambridge: Polity Press.

Fullan, M. (1991) *The New Meaning of Educational Change*. London: Cassell.

Fullan, M. (1999) *Change Forces: The Sequel*. London: Falmer.

Gay, P. (1975) *Style in History*. London: Jonathan Cape.

Gewirtz, S. (1997) 'Post-welfarism and the reconstruction of teachers' work in the UK', *Journal of Education Policy*, **12**(4), 217–31.

Gewirtz, S. (1998) 'Can all schools be successful? An explanation of the determinants of school success', *Oxford Review of Education*, **24**(4), 439–58.

Gewirtz, S., Ball, S. J. and Bowe, R. (1995) *Markets, Choice and Equity in Education*. Milton Keynes: Open University Press.

Gilroy, P. (1991) 'The loss of professional autonomy', *Journal of Education for Teaching*, **17**(1), 1–5.

Ginsburg, M., Meyenn, R., Miller, H. (1980) 'Teachers' conceptions of professionalism and teacher unionism: an ideological analysis', in P. Woods (ed.), *Teacher Strategies: Explorations in the Sociology of the School*. London: Croom Helm.

Gleeson, D. (1987) 'General introduction', in D. Gleeson (ed.), *TVEI and Secondary Education: A Critical Appraisal*. Milton Keynes: Open University Press.

Golby, M. (1996) 'Teachers' emotions: an illustrated discussion, *Cambridge Journal of Education*, **26**(3), 423–34.

Goodson, I. (1994) *Studying Curriculum: Cases and Methods*. Milton Keynes: Open University Press.

Goodson, I. (1999) *Towards a Principled Professionalism for Teaching*. Paper presented to the international conference on New Professionalism in Teaching, Hong Kong, 15–17 January.

Goodson, I. and Hargreaves, A. (eds) (1996) *Teachers' Professional Lives*. London: Falmer.

Gosden, P. (1972) *The Evolution of a Profession*. Oxford: Blackwell.

Grace, G. (1987) 'Teachers and the state in Britain: a changing relation', in M. Lawn and G. Grace (eds), *Teachers: The Culture and Politics of Work*. London: Falmer.

Gray, J., Hopkins, D., Reynolds, D., Wilcox, B., Farrell, S. and Jesson, D. (1999) *Improving Schools: Performance and Potential*. Buckingham: Open University Press.

Hailsham, Lord (1959) letter to Sir David Eccles, 22 December (Ministry of Education papers, ED.147/794).

Hailsham, Lord (1961) letter to Sir David Eccles, 10 February (Ministry of Education papers, ED.147/794).

Halford, S. and Leonard, P. (1999) 'New identities? Professionalism, managerialism and the construction of self', in M. Exworthy and S. Halford (eds), *Professionals and the New Managerialism in the Public Sector*. Buckingham: Open University Press, 101–21.

*Hansard* (1960) House of Commons Debates vol. 620, cols 51–2, 21 March.

*Hansard* (1987) House of Commons Debates vol. 123, col. 774, 1 December.

Hansot, E. and Tyack, D. (1982) 'A usable past: using history in educational policy', in A. Lieberman and M. McLaughlin (eds), *Policy-Making in Education*. Chicago: National Society for the Study of Education.

Hargreaves, A. (1992) 'Cultures of teaching: a focus for change', in A. Hargreaves and M. Fullan (eds), *Understanding Teacher Development*. London: Cassell.

Hargreaves, A. (1994) *Changing Teachers, Changing Times*. London: Cassell.

Hargreaves, A. (1995) 'Beyond collaboration: critical teacher development in the post-modern age', in J. Smyth (ed.), *Critical Discourses on Teacher Development*. Toronto, Ontario: OISE Press.

Hargreaves, A. (1998) 'The emotional practice of teaching', *Teaching and Teacher Education*, **14**(8), 835–54.

Hargreaves, A. (1999a) *Mixed Emotions: Teachers' Perceptions of their Classroom Relationships with their Students*. Paper presented to the international conference on New Professionalism in Teaching, Hong Kong, 15–17 January.

Hargreaves, A. (1999b) *Professionals and Parents: Personal Adversaries or Public Allies?* Paper presented to the international conference on New Professionalism in Teaching, Hong Kong, 15–17 January.

Hargreaves, A. and Goodson, I. (1996) 'Teachers' professional lives: aspirations and actualities', in I. Goodson and A. Hargreaves (eds), *Teachers' Professional Lives*. London: Falmer.

Harland, J. (1987) 'The TVEI experience: issues of control, response and the professional role of teachers', in D. Gleeson (ed.), *TVEI and Secondary Education: A Critical Appraisal*. Milton Keynes: Open University Press.

Harris, A., Bennett, N. and Preedy, M. (eds) (1997) *Organizational Effectiveness and Improvement in Education*. Buckingham: Open University Press.

Harris, A., Jamieson, I. and Ross, J. (1997) 'A study of "effective" departments in secondary schools', in A. Harris, N. Bennett and M. Preedy (eds), *Organizational Effectiveness and Improvement in Education*. Buckingham: Open University Press.

Harrison, G. B. (1968) 'Inhibiting influences on school teachers', for School Science and Technology Committee (SSTC papers, Nottingham Trent University).

Helsby, G. (1995) 'Teachers' construction of professionalism in England in the 1990s', *Journal of Education for Teaching*, **21**(3): 317–32.

Helsby, G. (1999) *Changing Teachers' Work: The 'Reform' of Secondary Schooling*. Buckingham: Open University Press.

Helsby, G. and Knight, P. T. (1997) 'Continuing professional development and the National Curriculum', in G. Helsby and G. McCulloch (eds), *Teachers and the National Curriculum*. London: Cassell.

Helsby, G. and McCulloch, G. (1996) 'Teacher professionalism and curriculum control', in I. Goodson and A. Hargreaves (eds), *Teachers' Professional Lives*. London: Falmer.

Helsby, G. and McCulloch, G. (eds) (1997) *Teachers and the National Curriculum*. London: Cassell.

Hesselbein, F., Goldsmith, M. and Beckhard, R. (eds) (1996) *The Leader of the Future*. San Francisco: Jossey-Bass.

Hinckley, S. (1987) 'Implementing TVEI: some teacher-related issues', in S. M. Hinckley, C. J. Pole, D. Sims and S. M. Stoney, *The TVEI Experience: Views from Teachers and Students*. Sheffield: Manpower Services Commission.

Hobsbawm, E. and Ranger, T. (eds) (1983) *The Invention of Tradition*. Cambridge: Cambridge University Press.

Holmes, M. (1945) note to A. A. Part, 13 August (Ministry of Education papers, ED.147/21).

Hood, C. (1991) 'A public management for all seasons?', *Public Administration*, **69**, 3–19.

Hoyle, E. (1974) 'Professionality, professionalism and control in teaching', *London Educational Review*, **3**, 13–19.

Hoyle, E. and John, P. (1995) *Professional Knowledge and Professional Practice*. London: Cassell.

Huberman, M. (1993) *The Lives of Teachers*. London: Cassell.

Jackson, P. (1968). *Life in Classrooms*. New York: Holt Rinehart and Winston.

Jones, A., McCulloch, G., Marshall, J., Smith, G. and Smith, L. (1990) *Myths and Realities: Schooling in New Zealand*, Palmerston North: Dunmore Press.

Joseph, K. (1984) 'Postscript', *Oxford Review of Education*, **10**(2), 147–8.

Kerr, J. F. (1968) 'The problem of curriculum reform', in J. F. Kerr, *Changing the Curriculum*. London: University of London Press.

Kliebard, H. M. (1987) *The Struggle for the American Curriculum, 1893–1958*. New York: Routledge.

Knight, P. T. (1996) 'Subject associations: the case of secondary phase Geography and Home Economics, 1976–1994', *History of Education*, **25**(3), 269–84.

Knight, P. T. and Saunders, M. (1999) 'Understanding teachers' professional cultures through interview: a constructivist approach', *Evaluation and Research in Education*, **13**(3).

Kolakowski, L. (1978) *Main Currents of Marxism: Its Rise, Growth, and Dissolution*, vol. 1. Oxford: Clarendon.

Lawn, M. (1987a) 'The spur and the bridle: changing the mode of curriculum control', *Journal of Curriculum Studies*, **19**(3), 227–36.

Lawn, M. (1987b) *Servants of the State: The Contested Control of Teaching, 1900–1930*. London: Falmer.

Lawn, M. (1996) *Modern Times? Work, Professionalism and Citizenship in Teaching*. London: Falmer.

Lawn, M. and Ozga, J. (1986) 'Unequal partners: teachers under "indirect rule" ', *British Journal of Sociology of Education*, **7**(2), 225–38.

Lawn, M. and Ozga, J. (1988) 'The educational worker?', in J. Ozga (ed.), *The Educational Worker*. Buckingham: Open University Press.

Lawton, D. (1980) *The Politics of the School Curriculum*. London: Routledge.

Lawton, D. (1993) 'Is there coherence and purpose in the National Curriculum?', in B. Simon and C. Chitty (eds), *Education Answers Back: Critical Responses to Government Policy*. London: Lawrence and Wishart.

Lazarus, R. (1991) *Emotion and Adaptation*. New York: Oxford University Press.

Levacic, R. (1995) *Local Management of Schools: Analysis and Practice*. Buckingham: Open University Press.

Little, J. W. (1992) 'Opening the black box of the professional community', in A. Lieberman (ed.), *The Changing Contexts of Teaching*, Chicago, IL: National Society for the Study of Education and University of Chicago Press, 157–78.

Lloyd, G. (1958) letter to J. Lockwood, 17 June (Ministry of Education papers, ED.147/304).

Lortie, D. (1975) *Schoolteacher*. Chicago: University of Chicago Press.

McCracken, G. (1988) *The Long Interview*. Beverley Hills: Sage.

McCulloch, G. (1987) 'History and policy: the politics of the TVEI', in D. Gleeson (ed.), *TVEI and Secondary Education: A Critical Appraisal*. Milton Keynes: Open University Press.

McCulloch, G. (1988) 'Imperial and colonial designs: the case of Auckland Grammar School', *History of Education*, **17**(4), 257–67.

McCulloch, G. (1991) *Philosophers and Kings: Education for Leadership in Modern England*. Cambridge: Cambridge University Press.

McCulloch, G. (1994) *Educational Reconstruction: The 1944 Education Act and the 21st Century*. London: Woburn Press.

McCulloch, G. (1995a) *Teachers and the National Curriculum in England and Wales*. Paper presented to international PACT conference, 'Teachers' Experiences of Educational Reform', 2–4 April.

McCulloch, G. (1995b) *Educational Reconstruction: From the 1944 Education Act to the 21st Century*. Inaugural lecture, University of Sheffield, 1 February.

McCulloch, G. (1997a) 'Teachers and the National Curriculum in England and Wales: socio-historical frameworks', in G. Helsby and G. McCulloch (eds), *Teachers and the National Curriculum*. London: Cassell.

McCulloch, G. (1997b) 'Teachers, Myth and Memory'. Paper presented to PACT network meeting, Oslo, 19–20 May.

McCulloch, G., Jenkins, E. and Layton, D. (1985) *Technological Revolution? The Politics of School Science and Technology in England and Wales since 1945*. London: Falmer.

McGregor, D. (1960) *The Human Side of Enterprise*. New York: McGraw-Hill.

McHugh, M. and McMullen, L. (1995) 'Headteacher or manager? Implications for training and development', *School Organisation*, **15**(1): 23–34.

Maslow, A. (1998) *Maslow on Management*. Chichester: John Wiley.

Mason, S. C. (1946) letter to R. C. Charles (Ministry of Education), 5 March (Ministry of Education papers, ED.147/133).

Menter, I., Muschamp, Y., Nicholls, P., Ozga, J. and Pollard, A. (1997) *Work and Identity in the Primary School: A Post-Fordist Analysis*. Buckingham: Open University Press.

Merson, M. (1990) 'The problem of teaching style in TVEI', in D. Hopkins (ed.), *TVEI at the Change of Life*. Clevedon: Multilingual Matters.

Millett, A. (1996) *Pedagogy: The Last Corner of the Secret Garden*. Third Annual Education Lecture, King's College, London. July.

Millett, A. (1999a) *Professionalism, Pedagogy and Leadership in our Schools: Raising Educational Standards*. City of York Annual Education Lecture, 11 February.

Millett, A. (1999b) *Developing the Teaching Profession: Meeting the Challenge of Change*. Lecture to QMW, 11 February.

Ministry of Education (1945) *The Nation's Schools: Their Plan and Purpose*. London: HMSO.

Ministry of Education (1947) *The New Secondary Education*. London: HMSO.

Ministry of Education (1955) internal note to Minister, n.d. [January], 'The New Secondary Education, 1947' (Ministry of Education papers, ED.147/207).

Ministry of Education (1956) secondary modern sub-panel, 11–12 April (Ministry of Education papers, ED.147/639).

Ministry of Education (1960a) meeting, 'Scientific and technical education', 12 January (Ministry of Education papers, ED.147/794).

Ministry of Education (1960b) memo, 'Revision of school science curricula: note by the Ministry of Education', 7 April (Ministry of Education papers, ED.147/1332).

Ministry of Education (1961a) 'Note of preliminary meeting on school science syllabuses', 27 March (Ministry of Education papers, ED.147/794).

Ministry of Education (1961b) Inspectorate secondary education panel (A2), 33rd meeting, 5 October, minute 8 (Ministry of Education papers, ED.158/21).

Ministry of Education (1963a) Curriculum and Examinations Working Party paper no. 4, 'Towards a Solution' (Ministry of Education papers, ED.147/814).

Ministry of Education (1963b) Curriculum and Examinations Working Party paper no. 3, 'The Outlines of the Problem' (Ministry of Education papers, ED.147/814).

Ministry of Education (1963c) Curriculum and Examinations Working Party paper no. 8, 'Pressures on the School Curriculum' (Ministry of Education papers, ED.147/815).

Moore, R. (1990) 'TVEI, education and industry', in R. Dale, R. Bowe, D. Harris, M. Loveys, R. Moore, C. Shilling, P. Sikes, J. Trevitt and V. Valsecchi, *The TVEI Story: Policy, Practice and Preparation for the Workforce*. Milton Keynes, Open University Press.

Morrell, D. (1964) note to L. Norwood, 8 May (Ministry of Education papers, ED.147/655).

Mortimore, P., Sammons, P., Stoll, L., Lewis, D. and Ecob, R. (1988) *School Matters*. Wells: Open Books.

Murphy, R. (1990) 'Proletarianization or bureaucratization: the fall of the professional?', in R. Torstendahl and M. Burrage (eds), *The Formation of Professions*. London: Sage.

Myerson, D. and Martin, J. (1997) 'Cultural change: an integration of three different views', in A. Harris, N. Bennett and A. Preedy (eds), *Organizational Effectiveness and Improvement in Education*. Buckingham: Open University Press.

National Curriculum Council (1989) *The National Curriculum and Whole Curriculum Planning: Preliminary Guidance*. Circular no. 6. York: NCC.

Neisser, U. and Fivush, R. (eds) (1994) *The Remembering Self: Construction and Accuracy in the Self-Narrative*. Cambridge: Cambridge University Press.

Nias, J. (1996) 'Thinking about teaching: the emotions in teaching', *Cambridge Journal of Education*, **26**(3), 293–306.

Nias, J., Southworth, G. and Yeomans, K. (1992) *Whole School Curriculum Development in the Primary School*. London: Routledge.

Nora, P. (1992) 'General introduction: between memory and history', in P. Nora (ed.), *Realms of Memory: Rethinking the French Past*, vol. 1: *Conflicts and Divisions*. New York: Columbia University Press.

Norwood, C. (1929) *The English Tradition of Education*. London: John Murray.

Norwood, C. (1942a) memorandum of oral evidence to McNair committee, 29 September (McNair committee papers, University of Liverpool).

Norwood, C. (1942b) memorandum to Norwood committee, 'The internal examination' (Incorporated Association of Head Masters papers, Institute of Education, London).

Norwood, L. (1964) note to D. Morrell, 18 March (Ministry of Education papers, ED.147/812).

Nuffield Foundation (1964) internal memorandum, 'Science Teaching Programme: agencies concerned in school science curriculum reform' (Nuffield Foundation papers, London, file EDU/52).

O'Hear, P. (1994) 'An alternative National Curriculum', in S. Tomlinson (ed.), *Educational Reform and its Consequences*. London: Institute for Public Policy Research/Rivers Oram Press.

O'Hear, P. and White, J. (1991) *A National Curriculum for All*. Education and Training Paper no. 6. London: Institute for Public Policy Research.

Osborn, M. (1997) 'Policy into practice into policy: creative mediation in the primary classroom', in G. Helsby and G. McCulloch (eds), *Teachers and the National Curriculum*. London: Cassell.

Ozga, J. (1989) *Schoolwork: Approaches to the Labour Processes of Teaching*. Milton Keynes: Open University Press.

Ozga, J. (1992) *Teacher Professionalism*. Paper presented to annual conference of British Educational Management and Administration Society, Bristol.

Ozga, J. (1995) 'Deskilling a profession: professionalism, deprofessionalisation and the new managerialism', in H. Busher and R. Saran (eds), *Managing Teachers as Professionals in Schools*. London: Kogan Page.

Palmer, P. J. (1998) *The Courage to Teach: Exploring the Inner Landscape of a Teacher's Life*. San Francisco: Jossey-Bass.

Perry, R. P., Menec, V. H., Struthers, C. W., Hechter, F. J., Schönwetter, D. J. and Menges, R. J. (1996) *Faculty in Transition: The Adjustment of New Hires to Postsecondary Institutions*. Winnipeg, MB: Centre for Higher Education Research and Development.

Peters, T. (1994) *In Pursuit of WOW!* London: Pan.

Phillips, R. (1991) 'National Curriculum History and teacher autonomy: the major challenge', *Teaching History*, **65**, 21–4.

Pietrasik, R. (1987) 'The teachers' action, 1984–1986', in M. Lawn and G. Grace (eds), *Teachers*. London: Falmer.

Pollard, A., Broadfoot, P., Croll, P., Osborn, M. and Abbott, D. (1994) *Changing English Primary Schools? The Impact of the Education Reform Act at Key Stage One*. London: Cassell.

Powell-Davies, M. G. (1963) letter to D. Morrell, 18 March (Ministry of Education papers, ED.147/812).

Power, S., Halpin, D. and Whitty, G. (1997) 'Managing the state and the market: "new" education management in five countries', *British Journal of Educational Studies*, **45**(4): 342–62.

Prendergast, M. (1997) *Victims of Memory: Incest Accusations and Shattered Lives*. London: HarperCollins.

Proud, D. (1984) 'Nothing but vinegar sponges', *TES*, 14 December.

Pullan, J. M. (1962) letter to HMI Mr Staton, 4 June (Ministry of Education papers, ED.147/755).

Reay, D. (1998) 'Micro-politics in the 1990s: staff relationships in secondary schooling', *Journal of Education Policy*, **13**(2), 179–96.

Roberts, M. (1995) 'Interpretations of the geography national curriculum: a common curriculum for all?', *Journal of Curriculum Studies*, **27**(2), 187–205.

Roberts, M. (1997) 'Reconstructing the geography national curriculum: professional constraints, challenges and choices', in G. Helsby and G. McCulloch (eds), *Teachers and the National Curriculum*. London: Cassell.

Rogers, C. (1983) *Freedom to Learn for the '80s*. Columbus, OH: Merrill.

Rosenholtz, S. (1989) *Teachers' Workplace*. New York: Macmillan.

Roseveare, M. P. (1955) memo, 'Examinations in secondary schools', 19 January (Ministry of Education papers, ED.147/303).

Ross, B. M. (1991) *Remembering the Personal Past: Descriptions of Autobiographical Memory*. London: Oxford University Press.

Rubin, H. J. and Rubin, I. S. (1995) *Qualitative Interviewing: The Art of Hearing Data*. London: Sage.

Sachs, J. (1999) *Towards an Activist View of Teacher Professionalism*. Paper presented to the international conference on New Professionalism in Teaching, Hong Kong, 15–17 January.

Sammons, P., Thomas, S. and Mortimore, P. (1997) *Forging Links: Effective Schools and Effective Departments*. London: Paul Chapman.

Saunders, M. and Warburton, T. (1997) 'Teachers' subject cultures: accommodating the National Curriculum in maths and technology', in G. Helsby and G. McCulloch (eds), *Teachers and the National Curriculum*. London: Cassell.

Schama, S. (1996) *Landscape and Memory*. London: Fontana.

Schön, D. A. (1983) *The Reflective Practitioner: How Practitioners Think in Action*. San Francisco: Jossey-Bass.

Schools Council (1968) *Curriculum Innovation in Practice: A Report by J. Stuart Maclure of the Third International Curriculum Conference*, 1967. London: Schools Council.

Seligman, M. (1998) *Learned Optimism*. New York: Pocket Books.

Shapero, A. (1985) *Managing Professional People*. New York: Free Press.

Shimahara, N. K. (ed.) (1998) *Politics of Classroom Life: Classroom Management in International Perspective*. New York: Garland.

Simon, B. (1991) *Education and the Social Order, 1940–1990*. London: Lawrence and Wishart.

Simon, B. and Chitty, C. (1993) *SOS: Save Our Schools*. London: Lawrence and Wishart.

Simons, H. (1988) 'Teacher professionalism and the National Curriculum', in D. Lawton and C. Chitty (eds), *The National Curriculum*, Bedford Way papers 33. London: Institute of Education.

Siraj-Blatchford, I. (1994) 'Back to the future?', *TES*, 24 June.

Siskin, L. (1994) *Realms of Knowledge*. London: Falmer.

Smieton, M. (1961) note to Minister, 24 February (Ministry of Education papers, ED.147/794).

Smith, D. and Tomlinson, S. (1989) *The School Effect*. London: Policy Studies Institute.

Smylie, M. (1995) 'Teacher learning in the workplace', in T. R. Guskey and M. Huberman (eds) *Professional Development in Education*, New York: Teachers' College Press, 92–111.

Sockett, H. (1993) *The Moral Base for Teacher Professionalism*. New York: Teachers' College Press.

SSEC (1960) *Secondary School Examinations other than the GCE* (Beloe Report). London: SSEC.
SSEC (1962) science panel, memo, 'Examinations in science for the CSE', n.d. [September] (Ministry of Education papers, ED.147/669).
Steedman, H. (1987) 'Defining institutions: the endowed grammar schools and the systematisation of English secondary education', in D. Muller, F. Muller and B. Simon (eds), *The Rise of the Modern Educational System*. Cambridge: Cambridge University Press.
Sternberg, R. J. (1997) *Successful Intelligence*. New York: Plume.
Strenski, I. (ed.) (1992) *Malinowski and the Work of Myth*. Princeton, NJ: Princeton University Press.
Sylvester, D. W. (1969) *Robert Lowe and Education*. Cambridge: Cambridge University Press.
Talbert, J. (1995) *Primacy and Promise of Professional Development in the Nation's Education Reform Agenda*. Paper presented to the 'Implementing Recent Federal Legislation' conference, St Petersburg Beach, FA, 8–10 January.
Talbert, J. and Perry, R. (1994) *How Department Communities Mediate Mathematics and Science Education Reforms*. Paper presented to American Educational Research Association, New Orleans, April 4–8.
Task Group on Assessment and Testing (1987) *Task Group on Assessment and Testing: A Report*, London: DES.
Tate, N. (1994) 'Target vision', *TES*, 2 December.
Tate, N. (1998) 'Core anglais', *TES*, 13 February.
Taylor, P. H. (1970) *How Teachers Plan their Courses: Studies in Curriculum Planning*. London: NFER.
Taylor, W. (1994) 'Teacher education: backstage to centre stage', in T. Becher (ed.), *Governments and Professional Education*, Buckingham: Open University Press, 48–59.
*TES* (1962a) 'Comment in brief', 16 February.
*TES* (1962b) leading article, 'Future tense', 15 June.
*TES* (1993) report, 'Patten "does trust teachers" ', 22 October.
*TES* (1994a) editorial, 'Deskilling teachers', 8 July.
*TES* (1994b) report, 'Test concessions halted', 14 October.
*TES* (1994c) editorial, 'Back with the teachers', 11 November.
*TES* (1998a) report, 'Pedagogue with a pugilistic streak', 13 February.
*TES* (1998b) report, 'Blair warns teachers not to resist reforms', 2 October.
*TES* (1998c) report, 'Tories tell teachers "we understand the pressure" ', 9 October.
*TES* (1998d) report, editorial, 'As good as we'll get', 4 December.
Thatcher, M. (1993) *The Downing Street Years*. London: Harper-Collins.
*The Independent* (1993a) report, 'Talk to me as professionals and I'll respond', 18 February.
*The Independent* (1993b) editorial, 'Boycotts and other distractions', 24 April.
*The Observer* (1962) report, 'The two million pound man', 29 July.
*The Times* (1983) report, 'Politicians well on way to controlling school curriculum, union is told', 5 April.
Tittler, R. (1997) 'Reformation, civic culture and collective memory in English provincial towns', *Urban History*, **24**(3), 283–300.
Tonkin, E. (1992) *Narrating our Pasts: The Social Construction of Oral History*. Cambridge: Cambridge University Press.
Torstendahl, R. (1990) 'Introduction: promotion and strategies of knowledge-based groups', in R. Torstendahl and M. Burrage (eds), *The Formation of Professions*. London: Sage.
Torstendahl, R. and Burrage, M. (eds) (1990) *The Formation of Professions*. London: Sage.
Tropp, A. (1957) *The School Teachers: The Growth of the Teaching Profession in England and Wales from 1800 to the Present Day*. London: Heinemann.
Turner, C. and Bolam, R. (1998) 'Analysing the role of the subject head of department in secondary schools in England and Wales', *School Leadership and Management*, **18**(3), 373–88.
Tyack, D. and Cuban, L. (1995) *Tinkering Toward Utopia: A Century of Public School Reform*. Cambridge, MA: Harvard University Press.
Wallace, M. (1998) 'A counter-policy to subvert education reform? Collaboration among schools and colleges in a competitive climate', *British Educational Research Journal*, **24**(2), 195–215.
Walston, J. (1997) 'History and memory of the Italian concentration camps', *The Historical Journal*, **40**(1), 169–83.

Waring, M. (1979) *Social Pressures and Curriculum Innovation: A Study of the Nuffield Foundation Science Teaching Project*. London: Methuen.

Watkins, P. (1993) 'The National Curriculum: an agenda for the nineties', in B. Simon and C. Chitty (eds), *Education Answers Back: Critical Responses to Government Policy*. London: Lawrence and Wishart.

Weaver, T. (1961) note to secretary, 20 February (Ministry of Education papers, ED.147/794).

Webb, R. and Vulliamy, G. (1996) 'A deluge of directives: conflict between collegiality and managerialism in the post-ERA primary school', *British Educational Research Journal*, **22**(4): 441–58.

Webster, R. (1990) 'Education in Wales and the rebirth of a nation', *History of Education*, **19**(3), 183–94.

Weimer, M. and Lenze, L. F. (1991) 'Instructional interventions: a review of the literature on efforts to improve instruction', in J. C. Smart (ed.), *Higher Education: A Handbook of Theory and Practice*, vol. 3. New York: Agathon.

Widdowson, F. (1983) *Going Up into the Next Class: Women and Elementary Teacher Training, 1840–1918*. London: Hutchinson.

Willetts, D. (1998) 'Blunkett's colonial rule', *TES*, 13 November.

Willis, S. W. and Dubin, S. S. (eds) (1990) *Maintaining Professional Competence*. San Francisco: Jossey-Bass.

Willmott, H. (1993) 'Strength is ignorance; slavery is freedom: managing culture in modern organizations', *Journal of Management Studies*, **30**(4), 515–52.

Wilson, K. (ed.) (1996) *Forging the Collective Memory: Government and International Historians through Two World Wars*. Oxford: Berghahm Books.

Withrington, J. J. (1964a) note to D. Morrell, 12 May (Ministry of Education papers, ED.147/655).

Withrington, J. J. (1964b) note, 24 June (Ministry of Education papers, ED.147/642).

Wood, E. (1999) 'The impact of the National Curriculum on play in reception classes', *Educational Research*, **41**(1), 11–22.

Woodhead, C. (1994) letter to *TES*, 15 July.

Woods, P. and Jeffrey, B. (1997) 'Creative teaching in the primary National Curriculum', in G. Helsby and G. McCulloch (eds), *Teachers and the National Curriculum*. London: Cassell.

Woods, P. and Jeffrey, B. (1998) 'Choosing positions: living the contradictions of OFSTED', *British Journal of the Sociology of Education*, **19**(4), 547–70.

Woods, P., Bagley, C. and Glatter, R. (1998) *School Choice and Competition: Markets in the Public Interest?* London: Routledge.

Woods, P., Jeffrey, B., Troman, G. and Boyle, M. (1997) *Restructuring Schools, Reconstructing Teachers*. Buckingham: Open University Press.

Young, J. E. (1993) *The Texture of Memory: Holocaust, Memorials and Meaning*. Yale: Yale University Press.

Young, M. (1958) *The Rise of the Meritocracy*. London: Thames and Hudson.

# Index